ISBN 978-0-484-61212-8
PIBN 10824632

This book is a reproduction of an important historical work. Forgotten Books uses state-of-the-art technology to digitally reconstruct the work, preserving the original format whilst repairing imperfections present in the aged copy. In rare cases, an imperfection in the original, such as a blemish or missing page, may be replicated in our edition. We do, however, repair the vast majority of imperfections successfully; any imperfections that remain are intentionally left to preserve the state of such historical works.

Abraham Lincoln's Contemporaries

Cassius M. Clay

Excerpts from newspapers and other sources

From the files of the

Lincoln Financial Foundation Collection

Cassius M. Clay's Speech.

We publish this morning a full report of a speech made by CASSIUS M. CLAY, at Louisville, Ky., on Saturday evening last. It is a vindication of the principles and purposes of the Republican Party, made before an audience of several thousand people, and listened to, according to the statement of our Reporter; with marked attention and interest from the beginning to the end. This fact shows that there are portions of the South in which freedom of opinion and of speech are not mere empty names. We cannot but hope that the people of the whole South may gradually come to see that they are far more deeply interested than those of any other section of the Union, in the calm and dispassionate discussion of the great social and political questions connected with the subject of Slavery. Such speeches as that of Mr. CLAY are admirably calculated to allay the irrational and passionate excitement, which has so frequently been invoked for the suppression of all debate, and the extinction of all freedom of speech and of the Press, in various sections of the Southern States.

The prominent feature of this address is its moderation and good nature. Mr. CLAY has earned a right to be heard on this question by the sacrifices he has made to his principles upon it. Living in a Slave State, where even HENRY CLAY was utterly overborne and almost ruined in his attempt to start a movement of gradual emancipation, he knew that the ground he took upon it would close the door of political promotion upon him for many years if not forever. He has sacrificed office, fortune, local reputation, personal friendships, personal security—everything that most men count dear, to his principles upon this subject, and to his devotion to that fundamental principle of American Liberty, freedom of speech and of political discussion. A man of strong passionate nature, he has at times been fierce, offensive and fanatical in his championship of his cherished opinions;—but he has always been frank, manly, courageous, and has commanded the respect of his most bitter enemies throughout the whole of his career. Time and experience have ripened his judgment and tempered his spirit; and he brings to political discussions now more of reason and of practical wisdom,—more that will conciliate and convince, with less that is calculated to exasperate and repel his hearers, than in his more youthful and impetuous days.

His speech on Saturday is an admirable performance. It presents the principles and position of the Republican Party in a clear light, and in most favorable contrast with those of the two wings of the Democratic Party by which they are opposed. He scouts the clamors of disunion, and rebukes, with just vehemence, the foolish and traitorous schemes of those who make them. The speech was intended primarily for a Kentucky audience,—but it is admirably adapted to any meridian.

CASSIUS M. CLAY ON THE CRISIS.

THE ISSUE DEFINED.

WHITE HALL, Ky., December 19, 1860.

My Dear Friend: Your favor of the 16th inst., advising me of a meeting of the people of the capital of Indiana, to take place on the 22d inst., and asking a word of counsel in reference to the pending issues of the United States government, which they propose to consider, is received.

I thank you most sincerely for this mark of your confidence in my judgment and patriotism. I yield to your request in a spirit of humility; but, I trust, with a fidelity and unselfishness which become one who knows how much all personal greatness is dwarfed in comparison with the magnitude of the events of our times.

The threatened dissolution of the government of the United States of America takes no reflecting man by surprise. The existence of two elements of civilization—of free and slave society—of freedom and slavery—of Republicanism and despotism —of appeal to right and rule of force—in the same government, was an anomaly in theoretic unity— was a disturbing influence before and in the formation of the federal Union. Thomas Jefferson and Roger Sherman and all the leaders of the true democracy looked upon the existence of African slavery as an alien and destructive element in our republic, and went down to their graves fearful of the issues which it now forces upon us—which are, in a word, to yield to its unquestioned rule or suffer a dissolution of the Union.

Before we can apply a remedy to the present ills, we must understand the real causes of the disease.

1. First, then, the personal liberty bills of the free states are not the cause.

The very dispassionate editors of the *National Intelligencer*, after a full review of the laws of all the free states supposed to nullify the Fugitive Slave law, admit that but four states have passed laws in conflict with the Fugitive Slave law, and one of them, Massachusetts, stands in a doubtful position. The intention of these laws seems to be simply to protect the rights of freemen generally, without reference to the Fugitive Slave law; and of but few of them to nullify the unconstitutional provisions of Mason's bill. Every southern state has similar Personal Liberty bills; and my own state, in defiance of the federal constitution, generalizes Governor Dennison's illegal refusal to return Lago into a law.

All the Republican party ask is to have that law cleared of its unconstitutional and insulting clauses and it will be carried out in good faith, as our fathers in the constitution agreed. And all Personal Liberty bills conflicting with its legal enforcement will be repealed.

2. Neither is the refusal of the Republican party to allow slavery to go into the territories a cause.

In this we follow the footsteps of our fathers; and the footsteps even of the disunion democracy running down to a late period in our times.

The South knows very well that, under even the local territorial sovereignty of her Cincinnati platform, by sad experience, she cannot meet free labor by a free ballot, and conquer. Her usurpation of political power in the persons of the Supreme Court of the United States, she also knows, as her great leader, Senator Douglas, admits, cannot avail her, even if acquiesced in by Republicans, against the inevitable "unfriendly legislation" of the free-labor settlers of the territories.

3. Neither is the election of Abraham Lincoln, the Republican President, the cause.

The South knows that Mr. Lincoln is a Kentuckian by birth, and has a Kentucky born wife, and numerous slaveholding relatives—that he is an old Henry Clay whig—a conservative by temperament, antecedents and avowals; and that all the constitutional rights of the South will be by him thoroughly protected. In fact, the leading minds in the secession movement now abandon this ground of offence.

What, then, is the cause of the disunion move?

It is simply a desire to rule or ruin—the old passion in the hearts of our humanity, which we are told is as old as the race, and antecedent to it, in the devils of old!

"The irrepressible conflict" between free and slave labor has been, by the natural laws of peaceable antagonism, fought out, and victory has perched upon the standard of Liberty. South Carolina had tested the thing as early as 1832-3. Failing in her designs of a separate existence, (by which alone she could compel some of the trade which centres in New York and the other free cities, into the building up of her own Charleston,) upon the Tariff issue, she has steadily abided her time, and now, as Andrew Jackson foretold, she takes hold of the slavery question to effect the same purpose, with the same disregard of the rights of others—even of the border slave states, but with more hope of final success.

In these aspirations of a separate existence, all the cotton states sympathise; with the additional desire of cheap slaves imported from Africa, instead of the high priced slaves which they are now compelled to buy of the border slave states.

Now, what shall Republicans do?

They can have peace by acquiescing in all the demands of the slave power; but it is peace at the expense of their equality in the government, and loss of their liberty! There may be some who, like Esop's fat dog, will accept the terms; but I, who, like his wolf, have not only seen the marks of, but felt the collar, will part company here! We can have peace by allowing the government to go into dissolution. Mr. Lincoln can say in his inaugural, whether issued from Washington or New York: "All those states which stand by the Union come up and take the oath of allegiance to the constitution of the United States of America and the laws made in pursuance thereof; and those states which choose, may peaceably file off to whatever new affinities may attract them." But look at our plains, our mountains, our rivers, our seas, and say how long would such a peace last! And lastly, we can have peace by standing on the constitution (and the laws of our fathers) as it was, is, and shall be, and making others do the same—a peace which will secure us safety at home and respect abroad—a peace which will continue the grandest development of civilization which the world has seen; and which, I trust, the Providence of God designs shall be lengthened out into the far centuries, when the sword shall be turned into the pruning hook, and the lion and the lamb shall lie down together forever!

But suppose the time has come, when the justice of God shall be no longer withheld, and the madness of slavery shall seek out its own destruction by a dissolution of the Union—peaceable or forcible—what then? Shall we give all as lost? Not at all. God rules still. If the cotton states go—they go to ruin, sooner or later! The grain growing states may stand by us—give up their slaves—double at once their whole property by the advance of real estate—by immigration and capital from the free states and foreign nations; or, if they prefer, keep their slaves with the same—or greater security in the future as in the past—subjecting their system to the economical laws, and advancing civilization till such time as we shall become a homogeneous nation; and all will still be well. But if double madness and folly shall send them off with the cotton states—still would the federal Union stand, with twenty millions of free hearts and free hands to defend it at home and abroad safely against a world in arms.

In such case we would seek by friendly negotiation with England, the union of the Canadas, which would more than compensate us for the loss of the South, and in turn we would stand the ally of England in her contests with foreign despotisms; and the two carry on the progress and civilizations of the nations in that union of sympathy, and race, and freedom, which only now slavery forbids.

I have thus hurriedly, my friend, given you my thoughts as they arise, without fear or concealment. Some have said that I ought to be silent—having just recovered partly from a long period of pecuniary embarrassment, brought on by devotion to politics—with a family which now especially demands all my care—with prospects of place perhaps, which for a quarter of a century my principles have made impossible—I am invoked, in the language of prudence to be silent. Standing in the vanguard of a great and dangerous movement—I am told that leaders of revolutions rarely survive them. I may fall by the hands of violence—may be driven into exile—and suffer poverty, and die in obscurity. What shall I say? What shall I do? I listen—I hear the voice of conscience—the voice of God—of the great dead: "The man dies but his memory lives." "Give me liberty or give me death!"

Well, then, I think old Ben. Wade's speech in the Senate is the true ground. Let us stand with and by him to the end. "The constitution, the Union and laws—they must be preserved." With old John Adams, "living or dying," I stand by the declaration. Your friend, C. M. CLAY.

J. W. Gordon, Esq., Speaker of the Indiana House of Representatives, &c., Indianapolis, Indiana.

Cassius M. Clay Battalion Defending White House, April, 1861.

From the Collection of Frederick Hill Meserve

Meserve No — 125
Fourth Supplement —
The Photographs of
Abraham Lincoln

61.5 TB

NEWS FROM THE NATIONAL CAPITAL.

WASHINGTON, April 16, 1861.

Some twenty years ago a gold headed ebony cane was presented to Henry Clay, bearing the following inscription:—

PRESENTED TO THE
HON. HENRY CLAY,
BY
HAMILTON H. JACKSON,
Of Brooklyn, N. Y.

In 1851 this cane was presented by Mr. Clay to his personal friend Colonel William H. Russell, of California, but a native of Kentucky. A few weeks since Mr. Russell presented it to Hon. Cassius M. Clay, who to-day presented it to Mr. Lincoln, knowing that he was always a personal friend and admirer of Henry Clay.

It appears that the administration has decided to renew relations with Peru, by the appointment of another Minister, thus virtually annulling and ignoring the action

Cassius Marcellus Clay

By J. T. Dorris

CASSIUS MARCEL-
LUS CLAY was born
in 1810 near Richmond,
Kentucky. He inherited from
his noted father, General
Green Clay, qualities which
made him a picturesque character in American history.
These paternal attributes, even
more manifest in the son, were
an unusual mental acumen, an
extraordinary physique, an
undaunted courage, and an un-
common fidelity in supporting
a worthy cause regardless of
opposition. At eighteen Cassius shared in his father's vast
estate, which included scores
of slaves and about one hundred thousand acres of land.
He received the homestead in
Madison County, later making
it famous as *White Hall*.

Young Clay early developed
a dislike for slavery, which increased after his entering Yale
and hearing speeches by Garrison and other New England
Abolitionists. On February
22, 1832, he himself had a
conspicuous opportunity to
declare his sentiments when,
chosen by the seniors, he gave
the only Washington Centen-
nial address delivered in New

CASSIUS MARCELLUS CLAY,
1810-1903

Noted abolitionist, orator, editor, duelist, statesman,
diplomat and soldier. Captain in the Mexican War,
1845-6. Major General in the Civil War, 1862. Minister
to Russia, 1861-9.

Haven. "And there," he wrote long afterwards, "I delivered my first anti-slavery speech." Henceforth he engaged his talent and energy in the cause of freedom.

After graduation from Yale, Clay studied law, entered
politics, and served in the State legislature. But he was
not always a successful candidate; and furthermore, his
support of abolition often embittered his opponents. Once
(1841) during a hot Congressional election he interrupted
a speaker to tell him that "'That hand bill' which he had
just read, 'was proven untrue by another of good
authority.'" Thereupon a political bully named Brown,
being engaged to insult and then kill Clay, called him a
liar and struck him with an umbrella. The way was
speedily cleared and the men prepared to attack each other.
Brown held a Colt's revolver and Clay clutched a Bowie-
knife. When at arm's length Brown fired at Clay's heart
and received in turn a powerful blow on the head. Fortunately the bullet lodged in the scabbard of Clay's Bowie-
knife. In the fight Brown lost an eye and almost his life,
being saved only by his friends interfering. True to
form, as soon as his enemy was disposed of, Clay raised
his bloody knife and shouted: "I repeat that the hand-
bill was proven a falsehood; and I stand ready to defend
the truth."

When Brown recovered, Clay was tried for mayhem.
Henry Clay defended him, and Brown admitted the con-

spiracy. The Great Pacificator
closed his address to the jury
with these significant words:
"And if he had not (done
this), he would not have been
*worthy of the name which he
bears.*" The jury promptly
acquitted him.

Mr. Clay persisted in exer-
cising his constitutional right
of freedom of speech and freedom of the press in the cause
of legal abolition. On one occasion when Rev. John G. Fee,
an ardent Abolitionist and,
with Mr. Clay, a founder of
Berea College, was violently
driven from a church in
Lincoln County, he immediately "made an appointment to
speak at the same place . . .
on the slavery issue." Prepar-
ing to address his hostile audience, "he placed a pistol on the
book-board," by the Bible,
"saying, 'For those who obey
the rules of right and the
sacred truths of the Christian
religion, I appeal to this book,
and to those who only recog-
nize the law of force, here is
my defense.'" Suffice it to
say the overawed audience did
not disturb him.

But later at Stanford resolu-
tions were passed threatening Clay and Fee with death if
they dared discuss the slavery issue there. Clay "at once
made an appointment to speak in Stanford." Thereupon
thirty citizens of Lincoln visited White Hall to advise
him not to fill the engagement. Clay's characteristic reply
was: "Gentlemen. say to your friends, that I appreciate
their kindness . . . ; but, God willing, I shall speak in
Stanford on the day named." Later in his *Memoirs*, he
wrote: "The upshot was that the courthouse . . . was
crowded to overflowing. The excitement was intense, but
I was heard without a single interruption."

Clay's speaking tour in the North for the Whigs, in
1844, won him national recognition. He was accused,
however, of imprudence in handling the slavery issue and
blamed for Henry Clay's defeat. Since Polk's election
indicated a loss to liberty, Clay determined to publish an
anti-slavery paper in Lexington. On June 3, 1845, therefore, *The True American* appeared, with "God and Liberty" as its motto. He defended his press until August,
when a committee, taking advantage of his illness, moved
it to Cincinnati, where the paper was published until the
outbreak of the Mexican War.

Notwithstanding his opposition to the annexation of
Texas, Clay commanded a company in the ensuing war.
In Mexico he was so considerate of his soldiers' welfare,

(*Continued on page 47*)

Kentucky's Highways Lead

Highbridge, Kentucky River. © *Caufield & Shook*

© *Caufield & Shook*
Three State Road, Cumberland Gap, Middlesboro.

© *Caufield & Shook*
Right: U. S. Highway 25, Rockcastle-Madison County Line, showing L. & N. Railroad tracks and highway marker in the foreground.

East Dixie Highway near Barbourville. © *Caufield & Shook*

"White Hall," home of Cassius M. Clay, Madison County.

Right: Monument over grave of C. M. Clay, in Cemetery, Richmond.

Cannon used by C. M. Clay, defending "The True American," Lexington, Kentucky, 1845. Colt revolver presented to C. M. Clay by President Lincoln in 1861, in appreciation of services rendered in defending the White House.

Right: Joel T. Hart's Bust of Cassius M. Clay. Now in home of B. J. Clay, Richmond.

On the new highway to Cumberland Falls from Corbin.

Nineteen hundred and thirty-one brought the grade and drain highway from Corbin to the falls. On September 7, 1931, this great scenic highway was dedicated in a wonderful grove three miles from Corbin on the new road. All State officials were invited; with most of the Kentucky State Highway Commissioners present. What a contrast —on this day, 2,785 cars from seventeen states passed one way across the new concrete bridge which replaces the old wooden structure, compared to the five hundred cars during the "Kiwanis Trail" dedication in 1927. Ten thousand people were present at the ceremonies. From September 5, to and including November 26, 1931, there were 13.975 cars going over the new grade, totaling 51,887 visitors (averaging 3.5 per car) to Cumberland Falls in this short period of time. Cars from thirty-seven states, District of Columbia and Canada were in this number.

Nineteen hundred and thirty-two saw the stone put on the new grade—thousands of tons, forever opening, the year around, Cumberland Falls to the world.

ticular names must be omitted, because there were thousands of heroes who gave their time and money towards the preservation of this great masterpiece of nature, it was the opinion of those present at this public hearing that here too a defeat was handed the park supporters. Nevertheless, no action was taken by the commission, but the matter was deferred until the coming Kentucky Legislature could have an opportunity to act.

A long and bitter fight came during the 1930 General Assembly of Kentucky. Weeks of sleepless nights were in store for both sides—especially the conservation group. Finally on the tenth day of March, 1930, after the House and Senate had repassed the bill accepting the du Pont offer over Governor Sampson's veto, Cumberland Falls was at last saved for posterity.

It will be recalled that the late Senator Coleman T. du Pont, a native Kentuckian, had offered to purchase Cumberland Falls and present them as a gift to Kentucky, solely for State Park purposes. This action of the 1930 Legislature expressed the appreciation of the people of Kentucky for this great and generous gift.

Cumberland Falls.

Cassius Marcellus Clay

(*Continued from page* 25)

saving many by his gallantry, that, on his return, Lexin
ton gave him a public reception and Madison County pr
sented him with a beautiful sword.

Clay helped nominate and elect Taylor in 1848; and
1849, he launched a "State Liberal Party" in Kentuck
In 1849 he killed a man, and, at the same time, was near
killed himself in a State constitutional convention ele
tion. His opposition to slavery and his approval of publ
education contributed to the tragedy. He was mention
for the Presidency and considered for the Vice Presidenc
in 1860. He supported Lincoln, who promised him t
war portfolio. In 1861, he organized a battalion of volu
teers, which defended the Navy Yard and the Whi
House until other troops arrived. "Lincoln issued
order thanking" him for this service, and also present
him "with a Colt's revolver as a testimony of his regard

In 1861 Clay was sent as Minister to Russia, but r
turned in 1862 to be commissioned major general of volu
teers. On disagreeing with Stanton and Halleck he
signed and returned to Russia in 1863, remaining the
until relieved in September, 1869. He always claimed t
credit for the purchase of Alaska in 1867.

After returning from Russia Mr. Clay continued
active interest in public affairs. He attacked Grant's a
ministration; urged speedy reconstruction; supported 1
Liberal Republicans, in 1872; but worked for Tilde
election, in 1876 and returned to the Republicans to s
port Blaine, in 1884. In 1848, his *Speeches and Writin*
edited by Horace Greeley, and in 1886, *The Life, Memoi*
Writings, and Speeches of Cassius M. Clay, prepared
himself, each work in one volume, were published.
Clay died at his palatial residence, *White Hall*, in 1903

HISTORIC KENTUCKY

Photos and Text by J. Winston Coleman, Jr.

WHITE HALL, MADISON COUNTY—This historic house stands about one mile south of the Lexington and Richmond pike and four or five miles from Richmond. Originally there was a two-story red brick house, the home of Gen. Green Clay who received a large tract of land for his services in the Revolutionary War. His son, Cassius Marcellus Clay was born here in 1810. After attending Yale University, young Clay, the son of a large Kentucky slaveholder, turned bitterly against the "peculiar institution" and became a noted anti-slavery worker. He established the True American newspaper in Lexington in the 1840's and later, during the Civil War served as United States minister to Russia. It was during his overseas stay that this house was built, and incorporated the older house in the rear. It was designed by Major Thomas Lewinski, a Polish emigre and noted ante-bellum architect and engineer of Lexington; the construction work was in charge of John McMurtry. "Cash" Clay, one of the most colorful men of his times died at White Hall on July 23, 1903, the same night that a severe electrical storm covered the Blue Grass and knocked off the head and shoulders of the Henry Clay monument in the Lexington cemetery. This view of White Hall, with Gen. Cassius Clay standing in the front yard, was made in the summer of 1894, by Capt. Isaac Jenks, a well-known photographer of this city. White Hall is now owned by Warfield Bennett, a lawyer of Richmond and a grandson of Cassius Clay. This picture is number one hundred and fifty in the Historic Kentucky series.

LINCOLN LORE

Bulletin of the Lincoln National Foundation - - - - - - Dr. Louis A. Warren, Editor
Published each week by The Lincoln National Life Insurance Company, Fort Wayne, Indiana

Number 1324   FORT WAYNE, INDIANA   August 23, 1954

LINCOLN, C. CLAY AND THE KANSAS-NEBRASKA ACT

LINCOLN'S POLITICAL REJUVINATION—NO. 4

Cassius M. Clay was Kentucky's most passionate and aggressive anti-slavery exponent. His father was a cousin of Henry Clay but there was no spirit of compromise in Cassius. On July 10, 1854, one month after ex-President Fillmore's visit to Springfield, the fiery relative of the pacificator arrived in the state capital of Illinois for an address on the Kansas-Nebraska Act.

He was cordially welcomed by Abraham and Mary Todd Lincoln as an intimate friend of the Todd Family. When Cassius was a student in Transylvania University at Lexington the main dormitory of the institution burned to the ground and the students found lodging in the homes of the people. Cassius, whose people then lived in Madison County, secured accommodations in the home of Robert Todd and here he became acquainted with their daughter Mary who married Lincoln. In a brief sketch of the early days Cassius said that "I was on very agreeable terms with the Todd family, who were always my avowed friends during my antislavery career."

Cassius Marcellus Clay later entered Yale where he graduated in 1832. He came under the influence of William Lloyd Garrison and imbibed much of the abolition philosophy of the reformer. He entered politics in Kentucky and was elected to the legislature. On June 3, 1845 he issued at Lexington the first number of *The True American*, an anti-slavery paper. Threatened by mob violence he fortified his office with two four pounder brass cannon, loaded and mounted them breast high in his office, wore a bowie-knife and kept a brace of pistols in the mouth of his grip sack which he kept at his feet by his desk.

The editor of *Lincoln Lore* while a student at Transylvania University remembers distinctly a story about Cassius Clay which William Townsend uses in his interesting volume *Lincoln and His Wife's Home Town*. This is the version used by Townsend:

"At one of the villages near Lexington, large posters announced that no anti-slavery speeches would be permitted under penalty of death. Some of the citizens sent for Clay and promptly, at the appointed hour, with his old gray carpetbag on his arm, he walked unattended down the center aisle of the packed court-room, mounted the rostrum and calmly faced the muttering, jostling crowd.

" 'For those who support the laws of our country,' he announced in an even, steady voice, 'I have this argument,' and he placed a copy of the Constitution on one end of the table. 'For those who believe in the Bible, I have an argument from this,' and he placed a copy of the New Testament on the other end of the table. 'And for those who regard neither the laws of God or man'— the speaker paused and fixed his dark piercing eyes upon the most threatening group in the audience—'I have this argument,' and he laid a brace of long black-barreled pistols with his bowie-knife on the table in front of him. Then he plunged, without interruption, into his speech."

Mr. and Mrs. Lincoln must have had some anxiety about the coming of Cassius Clay to Springfield. Upon his arrival the secretary of state refused him permission to speak in the state house which denial put Cassius in a perfect mental attitude for the occasion. The people assembled in Mather's grove where the present state house now stands. Clay first upbraided the civil authorities for refusing permission to use the public building and stated that "even in his own state—a slave state— the common courtesy of citizenship had never been withheld from him, no court-house or state-house door had ever been shut in his face."

The principal part of Cassius Clay's speech was on the Kansas-Nebraska Act and he concluded his argument with these words: "Strike at the monster aggressor (slavery) whenever it could be reached under the Constitution. . . . An organization of men of whatever politics, of Free Soilers, Whigs and Democrats, who will bury past animosities and, repenting past errors which all have been guilty of, unite in hurling down the gigantic evil which threatens ever our liberties. When men violate the Constitution, put them down. Repeal unconstitutional enactments, restore liberty to Kansas and Nebraska. Slavery must be kept a sectional and liberty a national institution, and then the Ship of State will again set forward in her glorious career of Constitutional Liberty."

Apparently the visit of Cassius Clay to Springfield greatly aroused Lincoln and later he prepared an editorial for the local press based on the Kansas-Nebraska Law which statute aroused every anti-slavery man in the nation. This is the paragraph which brought about the political rejuvination of Abraham Lincoln:

"That the constitution, and all the laws of the United States which are not locally inapplicable, shall have the same force and effect within said territory of Nebraska as elsewhere in the United States, except the 8th section of the act preparatory to the admission of Missouri into the Union, approved March sixth, eighteen hundred and twenty, which being inconsistent with the principles of non-intervention by congress with slavery in the States and Territories as recognized by the legislation of eighteen hundred and fifty, commonly called the compromise measures, is hereby declared inoperative and void; it being the true intent and meaning of this act not to legislate slavery into any territory or State, nor to exclude it therefrom, but to leave the people thereof perfectly free to form and regulate their domestic institutions in their own way, subject only to the constitution of the United States: Provided, That nothing herein contained shall be construed to revive or put in force any law or regulation which may have existed prior to the act of sixth of March, eighteen hundred and twenty, either protecting, establishing, prohibiting, or abolishing slavery."

We shall never know just how much Clay's talk contributed to Lincoln's decision to re-enter politics in the following month of August. In after years in referring to this visit to Springfield, Clay remarked, "Lincoln gave me a most patient hearing. I shall never forget his long ungainly form and his ever sad and homely face. . . . I flatter myself, when Lincoln listened to my animated appeal for universal liberty for more than two hours, that I sowed good seed in good ground, which in the providence of God in good time produced good fruit."

1959

Townsend's Cassius Clay Story In New Heritage

AMERICAN HERITAGE, t h e Magazine of History, June issue. Single copies $3.95.

William H. Townsend, Lexington historian and writer, is the author of "The Rage of the Aged Lion," an account of the venerable Cassius Clay's marriage to a youthful bride who lived at Valley View. It is a featured story in the current issue of American Heritage.

The community was scandalized when, at the age of 84, he took unto himself a 15-year-old bride. So aroused were people in Lexington and Madison County, Mr. Townsend writes, that they sent a sheriff's posse to "rescue" the girl, only to find Clay ready to meet them with muzzles of a cannon, a pair of pistols and a rifle. All were aimed by the bridegroom who boasted that he never had detained a woman against her will.

Hostile Welcome

When Cassius Clay returned to Kentucky from his diplomatic post as minister to Russia, he found himself in an atmosphere of hostility. Plantation owners held him personally responsible for the loss of their slaves, and his friends in the Republican Party left him in 1872 when he came out for Horace Greeley, Democratic candidate for president. The Ku Klux Klan denounced and threatened him when he armed Negroes and marched them to the polls to vote.

The Ku Klux burned his barns, stole his livestock and scared off his servants. With a revolver Abraham Lincoln had given him, he killed Perry White, who attempted to assassinate him.

People began to hear that he was about to marry Dora Richardson, the 15-year-old sister of one of his tobacco tenants.

Reported By Allen

A lengthy account of the marriage and events leading up to it, Mr. Townsend relates, was written by James Lane Allen, then a newspaper reporter. It stated: "The scene was a touching one, never before and never again to be equalled in American life. The strangely paired couple stood quietly expectant as the Squire thumbed awkwardly through his battered prayer book. A huge

White Hall, Cassius Clay's Madison County home.

stick of wood burned in two and the fire flared a little, lighting up the fine bindings of the book; gilded picture frames and exquisite copper engravings of Grand Duke Alexis and his beautiful Princess, warmly inscribed by each of them and presented to General Clay on their own wedding day, at which he was an honored guest . . .

"The ceremony was very brief, and when it was over the General gave his bride a vigorous kiss, which she bashfully but willingly returned."

The closing paragraph of the news story was:

"Some think the old General is crazy, but I do not think so. His mind is clear as a bell. I do not even think he is in his second childhood. But if he is, I shall have no fear of growing old."

Posse Arrived

Two or three hours after Allen left the house, Mr. Townsend writes, the sheriff and six of his posse comitatus, heavily armed, rode down the lane to White Hall. Hitching their horses they advanced under cover to the front of the house. The old General had been warned of their coming and he stood waiting for them on the piazza. He stood by a can-

non loaded with pieces of trace chains, horseshoe nails and broken horseshoes. Also he was armed with a rifle and his knife was strapped across his chest.

Addressing the posse, he said, "now gentlemen, nobody, not even my worst enemies, ever accused Cassius Clay of ever detaining a woman against her will. And, of course, if I may be immodest, I can say this, that nobody can say that they ever took a woman away from Cassius Clay, either. Mrs. Clay is up at the window. You are quite at liberty to talk to her. If she wants to go with you, instead of to remain with me, why that is entirely all right. I'll be very glad to place her in your charge, and you can take her. But if she doesn't want to go, then I can only urge you gentlemen, in order to avoid the shedding of blood, to depart, and stand not on the order of your going."

Shooting Started

Then the shooting started. At least 16 bullet holes remain on the piazza door, the Lexington historian writes. The General fired his cannon and knocked down the tree that the sheriff stood behind. He emptied his Winchester rifle and charged down the steps with Lincoln's re-

volver in one hand and his Bowie knife in the other.

In his report to Judge John C. Chenault at Richmond on Nov. 14, 1894, High Sheriff Josiah P. Simmons wrote as follows:

"Dear Judge: I am reporting about the posse, like you said I had to. Judge, we went out to White Hall, but we didn't do no good. It was a mistake to go out there with only seven men. Judge, the old General was awful mad. He got to cussing and shooting and we had to shoot back. The old General sure did object to being arrested . . . We come out right good considering."

For two and a half years the Old Lion and his child bride lived quietly at White Hall. Then Dora became homesick for her native Valley View, sought companions of her own age, and her aged husband put her in his buggy and drove her back to her birthplace, a sawmill village on the Kentucky River. In obedience to her wishes, Dora was granted a divorce.

The General spent his last days in solitude. Nearing 93, he took to his bed, suffering from the infirmities of age. A few days before his death on July 22, 1903, he expressed regret that his earthly departure was to be so distressingly prosaic.

A beautiful full-page color photo of White Hall accompanies the article.

The June issue of American Heritage is exceptional for its content and variety. Murat Halstead, a Cincinnati newspaperman at the time, writes dramatically of the Democratic convention at Charleston in 1860 when Southern delegates bolted to nominate John C. Breckinridge of Lexington for president. "Douglas, Deadlock and Disunion" is the title.

Lewis Thompson and Charles Boswell have written what purports to be a true story of the 1919 World's Series when the Chicago White Sox, one of the most brilliant teams in baseball, suddenly came apart at the seams in the games with the Cincinnati Reds.

C. G. Dickerson

Among Books And A

HISTORIC KENTUCKY

Photos and Text by J. Winston Coleman, Jr.

WHITE HALL, MADISON COUNTY—This historic three-story, 40-room house stands a mile or so off the Lexington-Richmond pike, about four miles west of Richmond. Gen. Green Clay, a Revolutionary War soldier, claimed the rolling acres which surround White Hall and, in 1798, built the two-story brick structure which forms the rear wing. His son, Cassius M. Clay, was born here in 1810. After attending Yale University, Cassius Clay turned bitterly against the "peculiar institution'" and became a noted antislavery worker. He established in Lexington The True American, a newspaper which was later suppressed by an angry mob and the type and presses boxed and sent out of the state. Clay was U. S. minister to Russia for six years and played a large part in the purchase of Alaska. He served for a time as a major general in the Union Army and took part in the battle of Richmond. It was during his overseas stay that this house was built, which incorporated the older house in the rear. Maj. Thomas Lewinski, noted Lexington architect, designed the "castle"; the construction was in charge of John McMurtry. "Cash" Clay was a wildly eccentric old man who mounted his brass cannon on the balcony, took pot shots at officials who came tax-collecting and, at 84, married Dora Richardson, the 15-year-old daughter of a tenant farmer. The old "Lion of White Hall" died here on July 22, 1903, during a severe electric storm which knocked the head off the Henry Clay monument in the Lexington Cemetery. Except for an occasional tenant living in the back part of the old house, White Hall has been empty and deserted since Clay's death 57 years ago.

Kentucky's Grand Old Lion

By JOE CREASON, Courier-Journal Staff Writer

He knew what he stood for, was outspoken in his ideas, and was an expert both with repartee and a Bowie knife

Cassius M. Clay (not the Louisville prizefighter) was one of Kentucky's sodbusters before and after the Civil War, as this story will tell. However, he never has been given the prominence many Kentuckians believe he deserves. By far the best work ever done on Clay is the speech referred to in this article, made by William Townsend of Lexington before the Chicago Civil War Round Table. The speech was recorded, and the recordings are available at $10 a set (two records) at bookstores in Lexington and Chicago.

HISTORY BOOKS overflow with evidence that the Civil War period produced men who by their deeds, courage and strength of character were truly giants on the American scene.

The list is long: Lincoln, Lee, Grant, Davis, Jackson, Morgan and countless others.

And there is a Kentuckian who, as the years parade past and as the characters who played a part in the turbulent times are studied critically, more and more assumes a place as a giant in an age of giants.

This Kentuckian is Cassius Marcellus Clay, crusader, abolitionist, editor, lawyer, Minister to Russia, Lincoln confidant, Bowie-knife fighter, fiery orator, patron of the arts and Union Army general who outlived all his Civil War contemporaries and, in fact, died only 59 years ago at Whitehall, his estate in Madison County.

Perhaps no other figure of the times was called on to test the courage of his convictions to the degree that was Clay; no other so points up the tragic emotional clash of the era as did Clay during his adventurous career of 93 years that spanned the slavery, Civil War and Reconstruction periods.

Clay's short career as a newspaper editor—which, incidentally, came to an end 117 years ago yesterday—underscores many of the characteristics which make him stand out from other men of the times.

Although he was the son of Kentucky's largest slaveowner, Clay became perhaps the most outspoken abolitionist in the nation, a stand which caused him to break with his father. The paper he founded on June 3, 1845—"The True American"—was started as a vehicle for airing his violent anti-slavery opinions. Lexington, then the hotbed of sentiment for slavery in the state, was picked as the publication site.

The opinions Clay put into print were so strong and so pointed that his life was threatened repeatedly. One threat was a letter written in blood and signed "Revengers" which read:

"You are meaner than the autocrats of hell . . . The hemp is ready for your neck. Your life cannot be spared. Plenty thirst for your blood—and are determined to have it."

Because of this and other threats, Clay reinforced the outside doors of his plant on North Mill Street

Continued On Page 46

Two of Clay's knives, designed for him personally, now belong to William Townsend of Lexington.

One of the cannon Clay mounted to protect his Lexington newspaper office from pro-slavery backers.

Cassius Clay as a Union major general in 1862. He resigned and became Minister to Russia.

In his old age, he fought off a posse

in Lexington with sheet iron and placed two brass cannon to cover the front entrance.

The paper continued weekly publication for more than two months until Clay fell seriously ill with typhoid fever. Then on August 18, 1845, while he was too sick to leave his bed, a mob called "The Committee of Sixty" stormed the plant, broke up the press and destroyed the type.

That ended Clay's newspaper career, but it only cemented certain basic beliefs: that slavery was wrong and must be ended, and that a man must be true to himself by holding to his convictions regardless of the consequences.

In many respects, Clay was a man of inconsistent extremes. Through his makeup was woven the thread of gentleness and violence, restraint and blinding passion. He was the breed who could woo Anna Jean Petrov, beautiful star of the Imperial Russian Ballet, one minute and the next defend himself with the skill of a true artist with the

bowie knife against disgruntled Russian noblemen. He did both.

Moreover, while Clay as a Yale-educated attorney, held deep respect for the slow legal process of law, he did not hesitate to clash with the law when he felt the occasion demanded. Such an occasion was the day in 1894 when he, then 84, fired on and dispersed a sheriff's posse that appeared at his estate to prevent his marriage to the 15-year-old sister of a farmhand.

"Nobody but a Kentuckian can understand Cassius Clay," said William Townsend, the Lexington attorney, story teller and Lincoln author who in all probability is the No. 1 Clay authority in the land. "That was told to me by Miss Laura Clay, his daughter, shortly before her death, and the more I have studied his career, the more I know it is true.

"I started the study of Clay 30 years ago with some prejudice. But I found I was wrong since he possessed qualities one is bound to admire. "Contrary to my original idea," Townsend continued, "he was not a bully. He never started a

Continued On Page 47

Kentucky's grand old anti-slavery lion, in a photo, probably his last, made at age 85.

Clay we... ld... on knife fighting

fight, but he was ver... pub... at the conclusion of many fights, including his last bad
at age 83 wh... three toughs broke into his
ho... ad... he killed two of them.

"A... for a Kentu... secmal... to law
no inte... for it in his othe... quality Kentuckians sup-
pli... his hi...

These qualities together with the fact that
he came back he... the son of a large slav-
holder, an labd l... man that he believed
in gradual equi... we... the this also
Clay that impressed me."

Another characteristic that made Clay st...
out in the roughes... tumble pol... of the
times. The vo... pol... out, was his gift for
the devastating repartee. In this regard,
he was even more lad... tha... his cousin,
Hey... Clay.

An example of that quick-wittedness occurred at Springfield, Ky., in the late 1850's
win... Clay was addressing a strongly pro-
slav...

"Would you help a ruaw Negro?" a heck-
ler interrupted Clay.

"That," replied Clay... "do... on wh...
wy he was running."

Another time Clay sp... in Slip... de-
gate a that... th... he wu... be killed if he
kept the engagement. Th... Courthouse was
packed as he walked do... the aisle ad
mb... to the rostrum.

"Now, gt... for those wh... respect the
laws of God, I hav... this," he began, placing
a Bible on the lectern.

"For tho... who res... the laws of man,"
he cont'd ... this...

"And for tho... wh... have respect for neither
the law of God nou... mu... I hav... these,"
said as he pile... two pistols ad a Bowie
knife blda... him.

The speech wet... off without interruption.

It is significant to point out that Clay wa...
a giant in mee...ways the cop... and con-
temp... He also was a giant physically, sta...
ing 6-feet-3 out weighing 215 pounds. He
wa... dar... with lvy arms, dark, flashing
eyes an... a vigo... of jet black hair.

Fix... of the day said he ... lost a ha...
and that that gra... back immediately.

In late... years, wh... the black hair had
tad... to whit... so reta... the name of
"lion of Whitehall."

Clay was born in Madison Clay ne...
Ric... on Oct. 10, 1810. His fath... wa...
was Green Clay, a leading ind... his
mother was Saly Lewis. After nine...
Joseph's Coll... in Nelson County, Clay entered Tra... College. Enter... he enter... to know Nay... Todd, the Lin... in who
home he bd... an... ma... hd... ted... and
over... wh... he was living in the college.

Although Clay in his sbp... was te... told of
slav... the old of slay... as a boy, it was
not until he transferred to Yale ad came
in cou... with William Lloyd Garrison,
the famous Abl... th... as he put it,
his "can hue... full of fire for slavery."

"As wat... to a thirsty wayfarer," he
ma... Garrison's arguments ad scale...
wo...

Returning to Kentucky in 1834, he lad...
aly has... the leading Abolitionist, and his
care... as a Bowie knif... fighter began.
So skilled did Clay eventually bd...
th... knif... that in 1809 he wro... a pla... 1
entitled "Ba... Techn... of Bowie Knife
Fighting." Among othe... dis... of the art
this graphic passage was included:

"Ba... Yes you sha... mak... up
your adversary is to obtain a headlock with
your left arm, and then drive yo... viciously
Continued On Page 48

Whether you are a Catholic or not,
you should know the truth about
the Knights of Columbus.

Is it, as some... rude...
secret society with designs agas... s
our government? Do its members
really take an oath to destroy non-
Catholic political power?

If such rumors were true, the
Knights of Columbus would nor-
deserve the friendship and esur...
of non-Catholic citizens, which it
is no more thoroughly patriotic
organization than this fraternal
order of Catholic men.

It is composed of plumbers and
lawyers, farmers and doctors, business men and scientists—Catholic men at every level of the social
and economic scale. Some are
rabi... I partisan on political and
public questions. They choose up
sides with all the freedom of any
other citizens.

The Knights of Columbus was
formed in 1882 by a small group
of the men of St. Mary's Church,
New Haven, Connecticut. They
had met at the invitation of Father
Michael J. McGivney, not to form
a national fraternal society, but
to "render mutual aid to the
members of the parish and their
families."

In the years since, the Knights
of Columbus has grown to more
tha... a mill... men... spa...
over the United States, Canada
ad oth... coun... of the Western World. But its purpose of
"mutual aid... and its principles
of Charity... fraternity and
patriotism...rema... unchanged
after more tha... 70 yea...

Millions of dollars ha... ber...
spent by the order for the relief of
victims of fire, flood and famine
...for the support of Christian
youth work... and to Chri...

education. In both world wars, the
Knights performed a service of
ministering to the spiritual welfare and comfort of the armed
forces regardless of creed, that
brought sincere thanks from a
grateful nation.

Nea... ly on... out of ever... six
Knights served his country in
World War II, and many laid
down their lives.

Despite these and many other
signal demonstrations of its principles, some people have the most
absurd beliefs and suspicions
about the Knights of Columbus.
This is due to the fact that the
people give publicity at times to a
false... g of Knights of Colu...
do... which has be... prly... to be
fraudulent, and which scores of
others have been forced publicly
to admit is untrue.

Messages such as this are published by the K... of Col. In
so that our non-Catholic neighbors
may judge us as we really are. If
you wish, we shall send you free,
in a plain wrapper, an interesting
pag... about this item... a...
society. And ap... will call on
you. Write for Pamphlet LC-9.

FREE—Mail Coupon Today

A hid gunman attacked him, and me

back of the left clavicle, thus severing the jugular. Under no circumstances must you then shift to the other walk as I l notic do before I became experienced. There is too much danger of hitting a rib."

The year after returning to Haky, Clay open d a law ffice in Richmond, and in 1840 he was elected to the State Sure from Man County.

ever did Clay let up in his relentless effort to end slavery. Her enemi s wer mle who could go to any end to silence him. This led to one of his cl s so brushes with death.

Clay's opponents sent to Nw Orleans for a professional gun named Sam Brown who had eer lost a bahe. Clay's enemies and had ed that he had been in 40 fights I ped for Brown to good Cly into a fight and then kill hi

He tried at a political rally at Russell afe, six miles from Lexington. At the peak of a verbal exchange between Clay and an pp o nent, Brown struck Clay with a walking ane. When he arose, Bowie knife in ahd, Brown was standing with a pistol aimed at his heart.

Brown walked until Clay was within arm's length, then fired. But then Clay was upen him and—as the indictment against him for mayhem read—he cut off an ear, gouged out an eye, split Brown's head and threw him over a low wall.

When the exciteen no was over, it was dised tt Clay had ed only a red wit over the heart. When he had drawn his knife, the bll had been lifted and his kn fe i Mt had been stopped when it struck the metal point of the scabbard.

In this u ile, razed in 60, Clay published his Abolitionist "True American."

A short time later ee the founding of "The Fre American" in ilien, and then outstanding service in the Mexican War.

er the war, Clay ered to his atislavery campaign. It was in this connection that he first met hin. The fendship of the two ed to the dent that, when el ded President, Lnln named him Minister to Russia in March of 861.

emained in Russia a year, then returned to become a major general in the Union Army. However, since Bowie knife fighting wasn't adapted to warfare, he resigned from the army and returned to Russia, where he ed as minister until 869.

Many years of active, stormy life lay ahead of Clay aft r b me ane back to Kentucky and life at Whl.

While he never has gotten around to writing the obk on Bly he has ight ut for so many years, Townsend all but did a book on the subject in a speech he gave before the Chicago il War Round Able in 1962. The epch is a classic, covering in dramatic fashion the over dtay and done in all the detail and humor which is a Townsend trademk. The eph was taped and more than 10,000 copies have been sold by the Chicago group.

One of the most fascinating parts of the Townsend speech covers Clay's marriage at age 84 to the 15-year-old sister of a farmhand. Townsend, in his speech, related the afternath of that incident this way:

Well, as Judge Lgn, x's law partner used to say, ere was quite an 'upsetle' in Richmond and bout this thing. So much so that Judge e ett con ded that the c eion quired the summon-

William Townsend, Lexington attorney and authority on Lincoln, has done much eh on the life of Cassius Ely. A eh of his hat Clay is ed in part.

off second best

ing of what then was he   as a posse
comitatus . . . to investigate.

"So it was that the high sheriff and six
men, heavily armed, rod down the lane to
Whitehall. . . . The old general had been
suitably warned of their approach because
his cannon . . . blad will pieces of true
men . . . He had his pieces of horseshoe. He had his rifle with him and his
Bowie knife was strapped across his chest.
. . . They got into a shooting match there,
his rifle and then charged down the steps
with a pistol in one hand and his Bowie knife
in the other.

"As to how that was viewed, I will red an
exact copy of the report will the high sheriff
mad to Judge Chenault:

"'Dear Judge: I'm reportin' about the posse
life you said I had to, Judge, we went out
to Whitehall but it didn't do no good. It was
a mistake to go there with only seven men,
Judge, the general was awful mad. He got
to cussin' and sabotin' and we had to shoot
back . . . I thought we hit him two or three
tips . . . but I guess we didn't. We come
out right get considerin'. I'm havin' some
misery from two splinters of wal in my
side. Dick Collier was hurt a bit when his
shirt tail and britches was shot off by a
piec of horseshoe and nails that come out
the old cannon. Jack wrenched his she
and shoulder when his horse throwed him
and we was gettin' away. Judge, I think you
have to go to Frankfort and see Bowie. If
he could send Captain Longmire up here wil
two light feelders, he could din   his men.
send some will the cannon ade   front of
the house, and the oda   and i   through
the corn field and up around the cabins and
spring house to the back porch. I think that
might do it.'"

The second marriage of Clay's lasted about
two and a half years. Then the girl left him
and returned to her home at Valley View.

Clay lived for six years longer and
was to know other adventures. As mentioned
previously, in the   of his life he
killed to   of three toughs who broke into
Whitehall.

The end cam for Clay on July 22, 1903.
Appropriately, the night he died, the wie
tornado on reed   struck the Bluegrass. The
Courthouse in Richmond was unrooled, light-
ning struck the statue of Henry Clay in the
Lexington Cemetery, tres   were hurtled
through the air like wisps of straw.

Tond   concluded his speh   these
words:

"And then the storm was over. The stars
came out. . . . The old general was asleep,
his last sleep. Lying on his back with a
favorite Bowie knife peeking out from under
his pillow, the restless, violent, stormy
spirit of the old lion of Whitehall had gone
to   its maker in the mightiest tempest
that ever Central Kentucky had known."

Clay was buried in the Richmond Cemetery,
and the career of perhaps the most colorful,
controversial figure in Ky   history came
to an end.

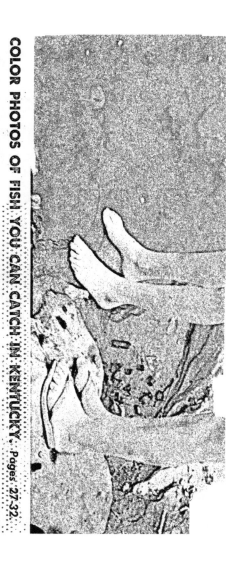

COLOR PHOTOS OF FISH YOU CAN CATCH IN KENTUCKY. Pages 27-32.

 A BRIEF HISTORY
OF BEREA COLLEGE

JOHN G. FEE

A BRIEF HISTORY OF BEREA COLLEGE

CASSIUS M. CLAY

THE FOUNDING

Three names stand out in the founding of Berea College - JOHN G. FEE, CASSIUS M. CLAY, and J. A. R. ROGERS. Native Kentuckians Fee and Clay were drawn together by their abolitionist sympathies, although Fee's convictions, as an ordained minister, did not permit of any compromise. This was not altogether true of the wealthy and politically-minded Clay. The drama that unfolded as a result of this fact makes Berea's early history an inspiring story of courage and perseverance.

After graduating from Lane Theological Seminary in Cincinnati in 1842, Fee went first into the hill country of Lewis County, Kentucky, where slave-holders were few, and established an independent church with a handful of members. Because his views on slavery were unpopular among sectarian Christians, he advocated a church with no other creed than loyalty to conscience and to Christ. When audiences were small, he took to his pen. The publication of his ANTISLAVERY MANUAL in 1848 brought him to the attention of Cassius Clay.

Clay's background was entirely different from that of Fee. At Yale, Clay had been converted to emancipation by a speech of William Lloyd Garrison's, and upon returning to his baronial estate in Madison County, he gave much time to writing and speaking against slavery. His ritual for opening a meeting was to lay upon the lectern a Bible, a copy of the Constitution, and a bowie knife: the Bible, he explained, was for those who believed in God; the Constitution for those who believed in man; and the knife for those who believed in neither. Almost every cabin for miles around him contained a boy named Cassius. Since slavery was virtually non-existent in the mountains he looked there for his natural allies - men who would stand for freedom. Through his influence Fee was invited in 1853 to preach a series of sermons in the southern section of Madison County, in the foothills of the Cumberlands.

Fee accepted the invitation, and so persuasive were his words that he was urged to take up permanent residence. Clay offered him a ten-acre lot for a homestead. An antislavery church, with thirteen members, was established. The following year, 1854, Fee moved south and built his house on the first mountain footridge, on the land given him by Clay. He called this ridge Berea, after the Bible town mentioned in Acts xvii:11, where men were open-minded.

A one-room school was built in 1855 on a lot contributed by a neighbor, William B. Wright. It served as a church on Sundays. The first teachers were recruited from Oberlin College, an antislavery stronghold to which the fledgling Kentucky community soon became linked. The visionary Fee saw the humble church-school as the beginnings of a sister institution, "which would be to Kentucky what Oberlin is to Ohio, anti-slavery, anti-caste, anti-rum, anti-sin." A few months later he wrote in a letter, "We . . . eventually look to a college - giving an education to all colors, classes, cheap and thorough."

The summer of 1856 marked a turning point in the friendship of Fee and Clay, which was to affect the course of Berea's development. A rift occurred on the Fourth of July, when Fee at a picnic spoke out uncompromisingly on the moral evils of slavery. Clay, undoubtedly influenced by the approaching presidential election and his own political future, took the line of moderation. Men went home in confusion of mind, but convinced of one significant fact: Clay was no longer the staunch champion of Fee and his "radical" Berea community.

The first chapel was a rough frame building, whitewashed inside and out, with an open belfry. Equipped with movable partitions, it served as both classroom building and auditorium.

Common School Report for *1855*
District No 16
Number of children between age of 6 & 18 = 5
Common School kept during the year 1
Three month continuance
Highest No of Children in attendance 24
Lowest Number 7
Average Number 19
Cost of tuition for each Child 2.50
amount of money rec'd from the State
during the previous year 50.00
Amount raised by Subscribers 10.00
$60.

The above was rec'd as given by the following trustees Ferguson Moore
John G Fee
J. G. Rempo

This revealing scrap of paper, preserved by Fee's youngest son, Edwin, shows the scale of operations during Berea's first year.

THIRTIETH
Commencement
OF
BEREA COLLEGE
Wednesday, June 24, 1896.

SPEAKING BY STUDENTS.... 9:00 A. M.
BASKET LUNCH.... 12:00 M.
VISIT TO SHOPS, LIBRARY.... 12:45 P. M.

AT 2:00 P. M. OCCUR THE COMMENCEMENT ADDRESSES
BY

Dr. W. E. Barton, of Boston

AND......

Rev. H. M. Penniman, of Chicago

Exhibit of Home Industry....

in west room of Ladies Hall, from 11:30 A. M. to 2:00 P. M. A first prize of $2.00, and a second prize of $1.00 is offered on each of the following articles:

Homespun Cloth for Coats,   Rag Carpet,
    "   " for Dress,   Knitted Socks,
    "   Linen,   Chair,
Home-made Basket,   Ax-handle.

Miss Adelia Fox,
Mr. & Mrs. John Kerby,   Committee
Mr. & Mrs. Frank Hays

Fall Term begins September 30th.
Winter Term begins December 30th.

STUDENTS' JOB PRINT, BEREA, KY.

4

At right is a corner of the shelter built for those attending Commencement exercises and other events. It was later enclosed and used as a gymnasium. Today the Tabernacle, or "Tab," houses Berea's theater and dramatics laboratory. The original posts are part of the present structure.

Slaveholders, who had been cautious in their opposition to the powerful Clay, now no longer feared to threaten Fee and his small congregation. In 1857 and 1858 the mob spirit raged in Madison County as war drew closer. Fee's life was endangered several times, but he continued his crusade for human rights, and the one-room school continued its session. His unfailing courage in defense of his principles is a precious part of Berea's intangible endowment.

Early in 1858, J. A. R. Rogers, a graduate of Oberlin College and Seminary, came to Berea to help carry forward the work. He, too, was aflame with the idea of a college. The short winter term in the school had already ended, and Rogers and his wife began teaching an extra term, a "pay school," although the fee was not a prerequisite. The term started with fifteen children enrolled, and ended with almost a hundred. A program of the exercises at the close of the second term in December, 1958, still remains. It includes two orations - one on "Modern Society" and the other on "The Scholar's Mission" - and a drama on Cataline and Cicero, evidence that a "higher school" was emerging.

In 1859, Fee, Rogers, and other community leaders drew up a constitution for a college in Berea, and arranged for the purchase of a beautiful tract of some 110 acres on the Ridge (price $1,750) "for the purpose of erecting the college buildings upon it, and for a town plot." The fundamentals of that Constitution remain the essentials of Berea College today. The opening words are still "In order to promote the cause of Christ." The aims are clearly stated in the first two by-laws: "The purpose of the College shall be to furnish the facilities for a thorough education to all persons of good moral character, at the least possible expense, and all the inducements and facilities for manual labor which can reasonably be supplied by the Board of Trustees shall be offered." "This College shall be under an influence strictly Christian, and as such opposed to sectarianism, slaveholding, caste, and every other wrong institution or practice."

It was providential that concrete measures to ensure Berea's future were taken before mounting hostility, intensified by John Brown's raid in Virginia, finally engulfed the community in December, 1859. Two days before Christmas, a group of 62 armed men rode into the Rogers' yard and served notice that the Berea leaders and their families had ten days to leave the state. When the Governor refused them protection, the exodus began on the seventh day. The intrepid little group, numbering 34, carried only their most necessary possessions, confident of their eventual return.

Fee spent the war years raising money for the future college. In April, 1865, he, with Rogers and John Hanson (Fee's cousin and one of the exiles), met to make Berea College a reality. During the ensuing year, seven more trustees were selected, the incorporation was carried through, a legal charter secured, and an endowment of $10,000 was raised. According to its first catalog (1866-1867), the "Berea Literary Institute" had a total attendance of 187, of whom 96 were Negroes and 91 whites. By the time Berea's first president, the Reverend E. Henry Fairchild of Oberlin, arrived in the spring of 1869, the campus included a chapel (divided into classrooms by movable partitions), with several frame structures clustered about to serve as additional classrooms and as dormitories. The first college class was registered the succeeding September.

The early story of Berea would not be complete without mentioning the assistance given by the American Missionary Association. During the 1850's, this organization had commissioned both Fee and Rogers as rural mountain ministers of the Association. In its annual report of 1869, three men and six women in Berea College were listed as receiving part of their salary from the A.M.A. Donations were also forthcoming through the publicity given Berea in the Association's magazine, the *American Missionary*.

THE EMERGENCE OF A
DISTINCTIVE EDUCATIONAL PROGRAM

PUTTING THEORIES INTO PRACTICE

Berea's subsequent development embraced the principles and philosophy of its founders. Created to educate the needy and deserving, it was from the beginning open to all. At first, the College Department seldom numbered more than one-tenth of the entire enrollment. The small tuition fee originally charged was discontinued in 1892, when the College's finances were somewhat less precarious and a feasible labor program was established. Berea, during the

Berea's second chapel, built in Gothic style in 1879, was destroyed by fire in 1902. In its stead was erected the present Phelps Stokes Chapel, built entirely by student labor, even to the making of the bricks.

approximately fifty years of leadership by Presidents Fairchild (1869-1889), Reverend William B. Stewart (1890-1892), and William G. Frost (1892-1920), strengthened its underlying philosophy by its significant strides in the areas of integrated education, a work-study program, and extension services. Its first commitment, too, was soon established; to provide an educational opportunity for isolated youth of the mountains.

NEGRO EDUCATION

For many years after the Civil War the student body was divided about equally between the two races. The success of this experiment in a former slave state during the days of Reconstruction may be attributed in large measure to President Fairchild. With great wisdom and kindness he guided hundreds of young whites and Negroes into mutual fellowship and understanding. In 1904, when compelled by the passage of a state law to forego interracial education, the College raised a fund of $400,000 to establish a new institution for Negro education, Lincoln Institute, near Louisville. When this same law was amended in 1950 to allow integration above the high school level, Berea College again opened its doors to Negro students, and since the Supreme Court ruling of 1954, Negro students at the high school level have once more been enrolled in Berea's Foundation School.

THE LABOR PROGRAM

President Frost was instrumental in the development of Berea's unique Labor Program. One demand he made of the trustees before accepting the presidency was that Berea "secure better opportunities than now exist here or elsewhere for self-supporting students to assist themselves." He stressed the need for "productive industry" which would be a source of practical training and income for the student body. As a result, the fledgling printing office was put on a professional basis, college farmlands were put into cultivation, the fireside industries and a woodworking department were established, a brickmaking industry flourished for a number of years, and the present Bakery and Candy Kitchen gradually evolved. Today there are 63 organized departments of labor on the payroll schedule, providing in many instances valuable pre-professional training, e.g., in the Hospital, on the Poultry Farm, in the Library, in the laboratories.

The evolution of Berea's Labor Program has been highlighted by: the creation of the post of Dean of Labor in 1914 to administer the program, under which students are graded as they are in their academic work; the requirement passed in 1917 that all students must share in the school's labor to the extent of ten hours a week; the construction of Phelps Stokes Chapel by student labor in 1904-1906; and the celebration of a College Labor Day in May of each year since 1920, when awards are made, contests conducted, and emphasis placed upon the significance of routine and manual labor in an all-round education. Finally, the Labor Program has tipped the scales in favor of countless young people struggling for a college education.

NEEDY MOUNTAIN YOUTH
BEREA'S FIRST RESPONSIBILITY

By 1911, the number of students seeking admission to Berea was so great that the trustees amended the Constitution to make the southern mountain area definitely Berea's special field; and in 1915 the College ruled that students from outside the mountain region would be admitted only in special cases. Since 1937, non-mountain students, including those from foreign countries throughout the world, have constituted about ten per cent of the total enrollment.

The gradual decrease in elementary and secondary school enrollment, together with the increase in College enrollment, further indicates Berea's sensitivity to regional needs. In 1920, when Dr. William J. Hutchins succeeded Dr. Frost as President, the Col-

Fashions in mountain climbing change, but the fun of Mountain Day, like the terrain, remains unaltered. This traditional College holiday, now celebrated in October, has been held annually since 1875.

lege was made up of barely nine per cent of the student body. In the past forty years the picture has changed dramatically. The elementary and secondary programs were gradually merged as conditions improved in the mountain schools. The present Foundation School offers a high school curriculum with ungraded classes for students requiring special tutoring to span the distance from mountain cove to college classroom. The Normal School, set up in 1867 to fill the great need for district schoolteachers, provided this service until 1931, when a college education became Kentucky's legal requisite for a teaching certificate, and the College's Department of Education took over all training of teachers. A large secondary Vocational School (1900 - 1924) was discontinued when it became evident that this training belonged within the high school and college curriculum. Under the leadership of President Francis S. Hutchins, who succeeded his father in 1939, Berea today has a total enrollment of over 1,600, with eighty per cent enrolled in the College.

THE EXTENSION PROGRAM

Organized in 1899 to send speakers into mountain counties, Berea's Extension Program soon encompassed many areas. From 1912 to 1954, Berea cooperated with the United States Department of Agriculture in its County Agent program and for many years provided office space for the U.S.D.A.'s Home Demonstration Agent. In the years between 1925 and 1950, Berea adventured in an "Opportunity School" (closely patterned on the Danish folk schools) for adults who could attend school only a few weeks a year. Some of these sessions were held on campus and some in the communities requesting the service.

In 1943, at the invitation of Kentucky's State Department of Education and the Pulaski County Board of Education, Berea College became a partner in a rural school improvement project. A Berea professor was appointed Coordinator. Pulaski County then had 111 one-teacher schools; many of them without a teacher's desk. In the first year, 103 schools were painted and traveling libraries from Berea were sent out. By 1946, county teachers' salaries had been increased by seventy-seven per cent, a hot lunch program established, and the services of a dental trailer secured. Most important, perhaps, the people in the county were made aware of their responsibilities and encouraged to carry an increasing share of the burden, so that at the end of five years Berea's help became unnecessary.

Traveling libraries established in the 1890's have brought books to isolated hills and hollows by mail train, river boat, automobile, and muleback. Today Berea's Extension Library Program circulates about sixty thousand books annually.

ROSWELL C. SMITH
1829 - 1892

A founder of the *Century Magazine* and *Century Dictionary*, Roswell Smith attended Berea's Commencement exercises in 1885. Impressed with the spirit, and need, of the College, he offered $5,000 towards a new building. Its cost, when completed two years later, was $32,000, almost all of which was given by Mr. Smith. Asked to name the building, he chose to honor Abraham Lincoln. The simple dignity of its architecture gives Lincoln Hall a timeless beauty. Today it houses most of the administration offices.

The Berea College football team of 1903. Berea today stresses intramural athletics. However, the College competes in intercollegiate basketball, tennis, track, and swimming.

Young ladies at work in the College Laundry. Today Berea's modern Laundry serves the entire community.

Two Berea College extension workers leaving campus for a trip into the mountains, 1895.

11

BEREA TODAY AND TOMORROW

Berea's history reflects drama and dedication. But the challenge ahead may be even greater than those met and conquered in the past. Berea's function in the space age is still to tap the human resources of one of America's neediest areas - the 230 mountain counties of Southern Appalachia. In a day of spiraling costs and rampant materialism the task becomes ever more complicated, especially since Berea realizes no income from tuition. Its work depends upon endowment, and on gifts from friends.

In recognition of the regional importance and high quality of its educational program, the Ford Foundation awarded Berea College a major grant of two million dollars in June, 1962, providing the College raises six million dollars from other sources within a period of three years. Berea was one of 21 private liberal arts colleges to receive this recognition.

Although Berea seeks to fulfill a regional need, its interests and contacts have no boundaries. Each year about 40 to 50 foreign students are enrolled. Berea students travel on summer scholarships for study abroad. During the summer of 1962, the Berea College Country Dancers, numbering 20, toured Latin America as part of the International Cultural Presentations Program of the U.S. Department of State. Faculty members are in demand for exchange teaching assignments abroad, and 41 members of the general faculty have lived or worked overseas. President Francis S. Hutchins has been a member of the United States Citizens Commission on NATO.

Berea is a symbol of hope, as well as a laboratory, for underdeveloped countries throughout the world. Educators from many of these countries visit the campus almost daily; some come to study. Lebanon, Paraguay, and India are among the countries recently represented by these special students, who hope to adapt Berea's work-study plan to the needs of their own countries.

Berea possesses a heritage in which many have shared. Some have served directly as teachers or administrators. Others have shared by contributing funds for Berea's advancement. Untold numbers have helped to spread the story of Berea's special educational opportunity.

Berea's future will depend on the personal dedication of its staff, on the generous support of a widening circle of friends, and on its continued leadership in helping young people to help themselves.

The Alumni Memorial Building, dedicated in 1961, offers a panoramic view of Twin Mountain. It houses a student lounge, snack bar, cafeteria, the Alumni Office, and conference rooms. This building symbolizes the ongoing development of Berea College.

 Prepared by Louise Pelton from: *Berea's First Century 1855 - 1955,* by Elisabeth S. Peck. Designed by Jane Harris, Berea, Kentucky 1963.

For further information please write to:
President, Berea College, Berea, Kentucky.

SKETCH OF A CATARACT

CASSIUS MARCELLUS CLAY, the firebrand abolitionist, in whom was a strange mixture of courage, honesty, pugnacity and the wild spirit of a crusader, was one of the remarkable figures of Kentucky history.

As a youth he fought his mother, his schoolmaster and a slave companion. The day before his wedding he caned a rival in the streets of Louisville. And at the age of 93, shortly before he was adjudged insane by a Richmond court, he converted his home into a fortified castle protected by cannon, under the hallucination that people were plotting against his life.

Turbulence was his constant companion. In 1841 he fought a duel in Louisville with Robert Wickliffe, Jr. Four years later he mutilated Sam M. Brown with a Bowie knife, a weapon that he habitually carried. In 1850 he stabbed to death Cyrus Turner; and in his old age he shot and killed a Negro.

Cassius Clay was wealthy and well educated; he was interested in politics and was a State legislator. Clay fought well in the Mexican War. In 1860 Lincoln appointed him minister to Russia. He was recalled in 1862 and was made a major general, but refused to fight until the Government should abolish slavery in the seceded states. He returned to Russia in 1863, where he remained until 1869.

Violently opposed to slavery, and refused the privilege of presenting his views in the state press because of their inflammatory character Clay in June, 1845, began the publication at Lexington of an anti slavery newspaper, the True American.

The majority of Kentuckians were in favor of gradual emancipation but the tactics of Northern abolitionists by propaganda and slave stealing tended to turn much of the populace against interference with slavery.

Foreseeing trouble for his publication, Clay converted his brick printing-office into a fortress. He covered the outside doors with sheet iron to prevent them from being burned, and mounted two four-pounder cannon on a table facing the doors. He stored a number of Mexican rifles and lances and placed a keg of powder to be set off against any invaders.

On August 14, 1845, a number of prominent citizens met at the Courthouse in Lexington and appointed a committee to request that Clay discontinue his publication on the ground that its continuance was "dangerous to the peace of our community, and to the safety of our homes and families." From his sick bed Clay wrote a defiant reply saying in part, "Traitors to the laws and Constitution cannot be deemed respectable by any but assassins, pirates and highway robbers. . . . I treat them with burning contempt . . . and defy their action. Go tell your secret conclave of cowardly assassins that Cassius M. Clay knows his rights and knows how to defend them."

In consequence another meeting was held four days later. A committee of 60 citizens was appointed to take possession of the press and printing facilities of the True American, pack them up and ship them to Cincinnati, expenses prepaid.

Acting in an orderly manner, this committee went to the printing office, where they were met by the mayor of Lexington, who informed them that their actions were illegal but the City authorities were unable to resist them. The committee accepted responsibility for anything lost or destroyed and proceeded to dismantle the press, pack the equipment and ship it all to Cincinnati. Clay's private papers were sent to him with a note giving a full account of the proceedings.

The following September Clay brought suit against the "committee of 60" on a charge of riot. The jury returned a verdict of not guilty. After the Mexican War Clay sued the committee again and was awarded $2,500 damages.

FROM COLLINS' AND KERR'S
HISTORIES OF KENTUCKY

"Kentucky All Over" will pay $2 and up for personal experiences it can use or true stories, with references if available. Address Edwin Finch.

Cassius Marcellus Clay: he freed his slaves.

in 1845 he published *The True American*, an anti-slavery paper. Foreseeing possible trouble, he fortified his office with two four-pounder cannon, Mexican lances and rifles, and strategically placed a keg of powder to be set off against attackers.

When the President offered Clay a brigadier generalship, Cassius told Lincoln he would not join the Army until Lincoln freed the slaves. Thus, according to my studies, Clay was ahead of Lincoln on abolition. After the Emancipation Proclamation, Clay did accept a commission.

Now, CHAMP, knowing the kind of Clay from which your name was molded, why not salute your big-hearted, two-fisted Kentucky namesake for his great battling for civil rights, by reclaiming the Clay name, thus conceding that what the world needs is more

—not fewer—Cassius Marcellus Clays?

Then you can share with the original Cassius not only the name, but also this entrancingly apt description that goes with it (in the Dictionary of American Biography; Chas. Scribners, New York):

". . . in him was so strange a mixture of manly vigor, unfaltering honesty, indiscreet pugnacity, and the wild spirit of the crusader, as to make him one of the most remarkable of the lesser figures in American history."

You are even more attuned to the first C. M. Clay than that:

Lincoln made his friend Clay the American ambassador to Russia. You, too, displayed ambassadorial skill when, in the 1960 Olympics, you told off a would-be Russian troublemaker during an interview: "To me the U. S. A. is still the best country in the world, counting yours!" ∎

He never replied — tho both of us then lived in Phila.

An Open Letter to Cassius Clay

By DAVID S. KEISER

DEAR Champ-Emeritus:
"Don't call me Clay! That's my slave name!" I heard you say that on TV several years ago, Mr. Muhammad Ali.

I have long been interested in researching Lincoln and his times, so I decided to do some sleuthing and ascertain what was what. When you recently decided to move to my town, the City of Brotherly Love, I thought I'd welcome you by telling the fantastic story I found.

More than 100 years ago a General Green Clay owned a lot of slaves in Kentucky.

When he died, a son named Cassius Marcellus Clay inherited the slaves and immediately *freed all* of them—including ancestors of yours, Muhammad Ali. A man and woman in that group of freedmen thanked Clay for his monumental kindness—for their liberation—by naming a baby after

him. That baby, my research indicates, was your great, great-grandfather.

C. M. Clay, the colonel's son, was highly educated and had a magnetic personality. He was Abraham Lincoln's friend and almost his vice president, as in 1860 he was second only to Hannibal Hamlin in the vote for nomination as Lincoln's running mate.

At another time he was nominated for the governorship of Kentucky.

When the Civil War began, Clay was in defenseless Washington. Being no military novice (he was a veteran of the Mexican War), he organized a 300-man military unit of bellhops, cooks, etc., to protect the city until troops arrived. Lincoln thanked him for "Clay's Battalion" by giving him a Colt revolver.

Hating slavery, Clay resolved to rid Kentucky of the evil, and

Muhammad Ali: take back the name, a researcher urges.

In Lexington 75 Years Ago

Cassius M. Clay Defends
Good Name Of Henry Clay

A Seattle (Wash.) newspaper, in a recent discussion and comparison of Henry Clay and James G. Blaine, made some slighting reference to the private life of Mr. Clay, the most serious imputation being that the great statesman gambled. A copy of the paper reached General Cassius M. Clay, of Kentucky, who responds in the following vigorous manner:

WHITE HALL, Ky., Feb. 15, 1893 — Your letter of February 6, inclosing an editoral cut from the Seattle Post-Intelligencer, headed "Blaine and Clay," is received. You claim to be an admirer of Henry Clay and are unwilling to believe some things they said about him ,and ask me as possibly the best living authority for information about the facts.

I knew Mr. Clay from boyhood, and began to be personally intimate with him in early manhood. We were remotely descended from the same ancestor and I was devotedly his political friend and followed him till we separated on the slavery issue in 1845. I am and always have been a follower of Thomas Jefferson, who, I hold, did more to mould our institutions than any American. Clay no doubt believed in this prophet of the people, and by his life service got the sobriquet of the "great commoner." When Carl Schurz wrote his "Life of Henry Clay," he paid me the compliment to send the volume to me for criticism, and he well sets forth the leading statesman of our republic.

He was born in Virginia, had heard Patrick Henry and other Revolutionary orators, but migrated when quite a youth to the new Eldorado, Kentucky—and made Lexington his home, and law and politics his profession, and is buried in that city, which he has made immortal. A shaft of Kentucky marble, crowned with his statue in Italian marble by Joel T. Hart, marks the place of his ashes.

STRONG IN ACTION

Henry Clay was over six feet high, with fair complexion, auburn hair, and the bluish-grey eyes which belong to the Clay family. He was slender in person, but nervous and strong in action. His head was high and swelling in the moral and intellectual region, much like that of Walter Scott, but, unlike Scott's, slightly receding from a right facial angle; but the right eagle, which he resembled in courage, for Clay was one of of the cranium. This gave him the slight suggestion of the the bravest men that ever lived. He had none of the development of the bulldog brain — but that higher intellectual and moral courage—which makes man the head of animal life.

Let us glance at a few of the landmarks of his life. Though he was not the author of the tariff system, he grew into its leadership where he remained to the end. His idea was not to build up great monopolies, but to increase the wealth of the common treasury against the extirminating war of accumulated foreign capital, believing and holding that, with our abundant raw material and educated labor, the period of protection and infancy would pass and we could, under free trade, hold our own against the world. So, in a new country, he increased the capital by the United States bank, but keeping even an acutal value of paper and gold and silver by convertible coin. He was eminently the father of the ways of commerce, the national interstate road, which ended on the Mississippi River, the great highway which he had by diplomacy at Ghent saved to the American people. "The American system" therefore was his child.

PLACE IN FRONT RANK

In our foreign relations he stood over the sentinel on the watch-tower — in favor of the independence and protection of the American republics against European domination: for free trade and sailors' rights against British claims of usurpation and tyranny over our seamen, native and adopted, and above all leading with the eloquence and fire of Demosthenes against Philip, the war vs. perfidious; Albion, who dared to reduce us once more to British colonial servitude. Clay took his place in the front rank everywhere. In law, in politics, on the field of honor, in the councils of the nation, before the great popular masses. He was a born genius and leader. He "went head" and remained there. With the great soul of a patriot his own fame was his country's glory, and his antagonisms were not contemptible personal "gladiatorial" onsets, but because he felt that not to be for Clay was not a personal want of fealty, but treason to the republic.

Envy and his dictatorial bearing prevented him from being president. He was the candidate of a great mass of citizens twice in real contest for that office, but in fact their only choice as long as he lived. Scorning the crooked ways of machine partisanship — preferring to be right rather than a dishonored ruler — he stood proudly the dictator of all public principles and policies from the beginning to the end of a grand and long life, and on his deathbed saw the "Omnibus bill," which he dictated, through rivalry and envy voted down, at last, in separate bills, made the law of the land.

James G. Blaine is lately dead. I have nothing to say against him, or even the company with whom he lived and died, for I do not set myself up as "Censor Morum." Nor do I see why Henry Clay, of all the greatest and most loved Americans, should eternally have his private life reviewed. The consensus of great moralists of all ages declares against holding the personal failings of men to the public eyes after they can no longer defend themselves. "De mortuis nil nisi bonum" was the generous apothegm of the heathen Romans. Lamar, replying to the puritanical Chandler's attack upon Jefferson Davis, said that it was the vulture, not the eagle, which thrust its beak into the rock-bound criminal of ancient fables!

CHARGES TERMED RIDICULOUS

The charges brought against Henry Clay of being a "gambler" are ridiculous. Mr. Clay played cards, as his contemporaries of the South did, with his equals in private houses-betting, it is true — (I don't gamble) as they claim, for the excitement. Look at the millions now invested in race horses — utterly useless as they are — the vast elite engaged in the amusement. Are these men, and women as well, "gamblers." I was thrown in early life with the first class of men and women in the nation, and I never knew a more "refined" man than Henry Clay. It is true he ever professed to be a Joseph, but Henry Clay was never accused of "profligacy." But considering how the Northern women wanted to eat him up in the Northern receptions, and that he had to close the doors when the multitude of women nearly smothered him with kisses, I should say that Henry Clay was a "chaste" man. If Henry Clay, who was a free drinker of good wines at dinner, was ever drunk on good wines or a "whisky drinker," to that extent is an absolute calumny.

Birney, like Clay, was in principle against slavery, but he fled from the dangerous field of contest, an exile into the North, and like all cowards cast Parthian arrows against the Clays, who stood their ground against this barbarism to the death. It is true that the malignant James G. Birney party in 1844 defeated Mr. Clay for the president, but they did through the most impudent calumny, declaring that Henry Clay was an ally of the slavery propagandists and false to his life avowals of universal liberty.

MALIGNANT FACTION

The Garrisonians were great-hearted and brave men, but were nonvoters and disunionists. The Birneyites were a malignant faction: and see the result. By their vote they defeated Clay, and under Polk Texas came in a slave state. They were then traitors to the cause of liberty. If Clay had have been elected Texas would or would not have come in, but there would have been no war with Mexico. They were then responsible for the Mexican war. Under Clay we would have had the chance at least of checking the spirit of slave-holding propagnadism, and set up the peaceful tendencies of the age in favor of Clay's life policy of liberty for all. The Birneyites were then the responsible authors of the civil war and all its calamities — and the end is not yet!

So the fame of Henry Clay grows with time, and the corrupt plutocracy of our times hate him for his honor, his courage, his patriotism and his immortal glory! Jefferson was the greatest of his times, Clay of his: then came Abe Lincoln, the greatest of all! Honest Abe: poor in purse, he was rich in all that is worthy of memory among men. He died a martyr for the liberties of the people, whom our rulers would not enslave! Since the death of Christ none of the human race has been more filled with the spirit of the Almighty God. His name and achievements will stand as a landmark in the ages, till the sun and moon shall shine no more and the stars shall burn down into ashes!

CASSIUS MARCELLUS CLAY
—The Kentucky Leader, April 21, 1893.

Lincoln Lore

April, 1975 — Bulletin of The Lincoln National Life Foundation...Mark E. Neely, Jr., Editor. Published each month by The Lincoln National Life Insurance Company, Fort Wayne, Indiana 46801. — Number 1646

THE VICE-PRESIDENCY TWICE BECKONS LINCOLN

by Louis A. Warren

Editor's Note: The history of the Lincoln National Life Foundation now spans forty-seven years. In that time it has had only three directors, all of whom are still active in the Lincoln field. Dr. Louis A. Warren, our first director, is ninety years old this month and has graciously consented to do this guest article for *Lincoln Lore*. Dr. Warren entered the Lincoln field in 1926 with a book, *Lincoln's Parentage and Childhood*, which Benjamin Thomas has called "the most thoroughly documented study of the Lincolns' Kentucky years." Thomas adds, "Warren is chiefly responsible for our more favorable view of Thomas Lincoln." Almost fifty years later, Dr. Warren is still making contributions to the Lincoln field.
— M.E.N., Jr.

Press, radio, and television, over the past several months, have been giving preferential attention to sensational stories associated with the Vice-Presidency of the Nation. The climax may have been reached in a meticulous investigation by Congress into the private life of the recently installed incumbent. With the public eye still focused on this controversial office, it would appear to be a favorable time to observe how Abraham Lincoln reacted upon twice being recommended as a candidate for the next to the highest office in our political system.

The unimpressive status of the position through the years is well set forth in the December, 1974, issue of *American History Illustrated,* under the abridged title, "Forgotten Men." This publication of the National Historical Society calls attention to the forty Vice-Presi-

dents who have occupied the office up to August, 1974. Thirteen of them were elevated to the Presidency, and seven others were selected who will be remembered for episodes unrelated to the office routine. The remaining twenty, or one half the total number of the men occupying this high station, were grouped in a category described as, "men past-recollection."

From the Lincoln National Life Foundation

This lithograph of "Abraham Lincoln" from a photograph by Hesler bears the imprint of E. H. Brown, Del & Sc, Chicago. On the lower margin there is a pencil notation by George William Curtis: "These prints were showered through the Wigwam immediately after Mr. Lincoln's nomination May 1860. (Geo. Wm. Curtis)." The Lincoln National Life Foundation also owns another print of this same lithograph which carries a notation in ink by John G. Nicolay: "The above was circulated in Chicago on the day of Lincoln's first nomination for President." These are the only two known examples of this lithograph in existence.

One commentator, on referring to the insignificance of the position, referred to it as a "sinecure," which, according to Webster, is "an office or position of value which involves little or no responsibility or service." One authority refers to the holder of the title as, "A second-rate man agreeable to the wire pullers, always smuggled in."

Occasionally, during the past few years, the advancement of the Vice-President to the Presidency through constitutional procedure has occurred. This has had a tendency to make the office seem more desirable than heretofore. The recent appointment to the Vice-Presidency of a well known statesman of recognized ability, a member of one of America's first families, may suggest a revision of the public opinion about the status of the formerly unwanted office. Certainly it will be more inviting to the political aspirants.

Before this new appraisal of the seat is accepted, it is important that it should be reviewed in retrospect to appreciate more fully how Abraham Lincoln, fortunately, escaped the ordeal of the ice-Presidency. The earliest threat was at the first National Republican Convention in Philadelphia in 1856 and once again at the convocation in the Chicago Wigwam in 1860.

Abraham Lincoln's political rebirth occurred about five years after he had served a term in Congress. His return to the political forum is recorded in a third-person autobiographical sketch: "In 1854, his profession had almost superseded the thought of politics in his mind, when the repeal of the Missouri compromise aroused him as he had never been before." Inasmuch as the repeal was passed by the Senate on March 5, 1854, and subsequently signed by the President, it was called the birthday of the newly organized Republican party. The official birthday was later established as July 6, 1854.

An observer's account of Lincoln's return to the political scene is recorded by Richard Yates, at what is known as "The Springfield Jubilee," celebrating the Republican victories in 1860. "I had spoken and voted against the repeal of the Missouri Compromise, and when on my return home at the close of the long session of 1854, having published a card that I would not be a candidate for re-election, I was met at the depot in Springfield by Mr. Lincoln. He said I had taken the right course on this question, and though he could not promise me success in a district so largely against us, yet he hoped for the sake of the principle, I would run, and if I would, he would take the stump in my behalf."

Lincoln briefly referred to the original Compromise in these words: "At length a compromise was made, in which, like all compromises, both sides yielded something. It was a law passed on the 6th day of March, 1820, providing that Missouri might come into the Union *with* slavery, but that in all the remaining part of the territory purchased of France, which lies north of 36 degrees and 30 minutes north latitude, slavery should never be permitted."

Four months after Lincoln had been awakened by its repeal and had again entered the political arena, another incident occurred which greatly stimulated his newly acquired interest in the "No Extension of Slavery" movement. On July 10, 1854, Cassius Marcellus Clay of Lexington, Kentucky, a relative of Henry Clay, paid a visit to Springfield. The presence of the anti-slavery exponent in the capital city must have aroused in Mary Todd Lincoln many reminiscences of her early Lexington days. While Cassius was attending Transylvania University in Lexington, the dormitory burned and Cassius was one of the students who found temporary lodging in the Todd home. He stated on one occasion: "I was on very agreeable terms with the Todd Family, who were always my avowed friends during my antislavery career." He later graduated from Yale, and, while in New Haven, he was greatly influenced by William Lloyd Garrison and became an exponent of the abolitionist's philosophy. Later, at Lexington, a month before his visit to Springfield, he established an anti-slavery newspaper called *The True American*.

Upon Clay's visit to Springfield, the Secretary of State refused him permission to speak in the State House. Cassius responded that even in his own state — a slave state — the common courtesy of citizenship had never been withheld from him; no court-house or state-house door had ever been shut in his face. He gave his speech in Mather's Grove. This rebuff recalls an incident which illustrates the dynamic personality of Cassius Clay.

A Kentucky town in which he was to speak posted warnings that "no anti-slavery speeches will be permitted under penalty of death." Upon Clay's arrival, says William H. Townsend in *Lincoln and His Wife's Home Town*, "he walked unattended down the center aisle of the packed court-room, mounted the rostrum and calmly faced the muttering, jostling crowd." These were his introductory remarks: "'For those who support the laws of the country,' he announced in an even, steady voice, 'I have this argument,' and he placed a copy of the Constitution on one end of the table. 'For those who believe in the Bible, I have an argument from this,' and he placed a copy of the New Testament on the other end of the table. 'And for those who regard neither the laws of God or man I have this argument,' and he laid a brace of long black-barreled pistols with his bowie-knife on the table in front of him. Then he plunged, without interruption, into his speech."

Sometime after Clay returned from the Springfield visit he remarked: "Lincoln gave me a most patient hearing. I shall never forget his long, ungainly form, and his ever sad and homely face. . . . I flatter myself, when [I recall how] Lincoln listened to my animated appeals for universal liberty for more than two hours, that I sowed seed in good ground, which in the providence of God produced in time good fruit."

The Illinois contingent of the newly organized party was somewhat tardy in perfecting the state organization, but on May 29, 1856, a state convention was called to meet at Bloomington. Among the many speeches made, the closing address by Lincoln was easily the feature of the day and possibly his most eloquent declaration during his Illinois years. It became known as "The Lost Speech," inasmuch as the reporters became entranced by his oratory and no one of them made an available recording of it.

The Washington press on January 17, 1856, published a call to "The Republicans of the Union to meet at Pittsburg on the 22nd. of February, for the purpose of perfecting a national organization." Another incentive was "the providing for a National Delegate Convention of the Republican Party on a subsequent date, to nominate candidates for the Presidency and Vice-Presidency." There was also released an urgent appeal to take a stand on "the only great issue now before the Country—slavery or freedom."

Nineteen days after the Illinois convocation at Bloomington, the national convention opened its sessions at Philadelphia on Tuesday, June 17, 1856. The permanent chairman was Colonel Henry S. Lane of Indiana. John C. Fremont of California was chosen as the Presidential nominee on the first ballot. The chief order of business for the second day was the selection of a candidate for the Vice-Presidency. The trial ballot for the nomination recorded these several aspirants with the total number of votes each one received: William L. Dayton, New Jersey, 253; Nathaniel P. Banks, Massachusetts, 46; Abraham Lincoln, Illinois, 110; David Wilmot, Pennslyvania, 43; John A. King, New York, 9; Charles Sumner, Massachusetts, 35; Lieut. Thomas Ford, Ohio, 7; Cassius M. Clay, Kentucky, 3; Jacob Collamer, Vermont, 15; Joshua R. Giddings, Ohio, 2; Whitfield S. Johnson, New Jersey, 2; Henry C. Carey, Pennsylvania, 3; Aaron S. Pennington, New Jersey, 1; Henry Wilson, Massachusetts, 1; Gen. Samuel C. Pomeroy, Kansas, 8. It will be observed that Dayton received less than one half the total votes, while Lincoln was given twice as many votes as any of the other participating candidates.

A Pennsylvania delegate, John Allison, placed Lincoln's name in nomination, but, when the totals showed a majority of the votes were cast for Dayton, in order to reach a unanimous choice, Lincoln's name was withdrawn, followed by all of the other competitors. During the nominating speeches, Lincoln received many complimentary comments. It was an honor indeed to be the runner-up and a popular candidate for the Vice-Presidential nomination at the first national convention of the newly organized Republican party.

One of the stories of how Lincoln was first informed about the results of the voting, associates him with David Davis, the presiding judge on the Eighth Judicial Circuit of Illinois, where Lincoln practiced law. Davis was at the hotel in the town where the court was in session, when the mail arrived with news from the convention. He observed Lincoln coming down the street which caused him frantically to wave the paper reporting that Lincoln had received 110 votes for the Vice-Presidency at the convention. When Lincoln arrived and was given the information, he commented: "I reckon that ain't me; there's another great man in Massachusetts named Lincoln, and I reckon it's him." But, he was mistaken.

Seven years earlier Lincoln had visited the Bay State where he had spoken in favor of Zachary Taylor, Whig candidate for the Presidency. His schedule brought him to Worcester on September 13, 1848, where he was entertained at dinner in the home of Levi Lincoln, mayor of the city, and the Governor of the State from 1825 to 1834. Several distinguished guests were present and one of them recalled: "I well remember the jokes between Governor Lincoln and Abraham Lincoln as to their presumed relationship." At last the latter said: "I *hope* we belong, as the Scotch say, to the same clan; but I *know* one thing, and that is, that we are both good Whigs."

This episode recalls a visit which the author made to this same house in which Abraham Lincoln was entertained. My host, Waldo Lincoln, grandson of Levi Lincoln, mentioned at dinner that I was seated in the same position at the table, possibly in the same chair, which Abraham Lincoln had occupied, when a guest in 1848. It was the above mentioned Waldo

he exhaustive genealogy of the Lin-
e relationship of the Illinois and the
ts, branches. Abraham had properly
great man in Massachusetts named
y ancestral and personal references,
ladelphia for a final comment.
aham's complete surprise and appar-
identity of the Lincoln who had been
al ballot at Philadelphia, that he was
wide plans, then underway or pre-
is name among the candidates for the
ation in 1856. While his term in Con-
ignificance, the beckoning gesture for
lifted him out of local politics and
f nationwide attention. He could now
ding Western representative of the
lican party.
ognitions of leadership was revealed
of 1858, which named him, "The first
at in the United States Senate." His
ich clearly set forth the issue for the
ecame known as "The House Divided
because of his startling premise, "A
tself cannot stand."
contest, Stephen A. Douglas, was
he series of debates arranged attrac-
cal America. Recognizing Douglas as
eal of the Missouri Compromise and
stern spokesman for the "No Exten-
gent, the contest became something
bat. While Lincoln failed to gain the
oll the larger number of popular votes
' as the leading Westerner opposed to
r.

e, because of his solid arguments
ured for him serious consideration for
ticket of his party in the next Repub-
of the earliest feelers which arrived
has J. Pickett of Rock Island, suggest-
inois put Lincoln forward for the Presi-
ites. On April 16, 1859, Lincoln replied
llows: ". . . I do not think myself fit for
nly am flattered, and gratified, that
hink of me in that connection. . . ."
at the Philadelphia Convention, he
"fit" for the Vice-Presidency.
ished in 1859, presenting the names of
ontestants in the presidential race of
V. Bartlett with the title, Presidential
enty-one prospective contenders. The
ge with the caption, Our Living Repre-
thirty-four qualified leaders. It is note-
ublished Savage book named all of the
two exceptions. This combined list of
serve as a political "Who's Who" for
with party affiliations noted:.
Minor Botts, John C. Breckenridge,
well Cobb, Caleb Cushing, George M.
vis, Daniel S. Dickinson, Stephen A.
uthrie, James H. Hammond, Sam
nter, Andrew Johnson, Joseph Lane,
l. Read, Horatio Seymour, John Slidell,
ns, Henry A. Wise.
ion: John Bell, John J. Crittenden,
lard Fillmore.
aniel P. Banks, Edward Bates, Simon
'. Chase, William L. Dayton, John C.
ile, John McLean, William H. Seward,

, E. Wool.
the name of Lincoln is missing, as the
ared before his name became pro-
i address at Cooper Union in New York
1860, and the subsequent trip to New
d as his introduction to that section of
per Union Address before the Young
on of New York is accepted as the most
al address which he had given up to

for the Presidency in 1860 was Simon

Cameron, a Senator from Pennsylvania. As early as October
14, W.E. Fraser, one of his supporters, wrote to Lincoln pro-
posing a Cameron-Lincoln combination for the Republican
ticket. On November 1, 1859, Lincoln replied: ". . . I shall be
heartily for it, *after* it shall have been fairly nominated by a
Republican national convention. . . ." This statement documents the assertion, that he was not irresponsive to being
named as a Vice-Presidential candidate, but the reply also left
open the opportunity for an ultimate decision before the convention was called to order. Lincoln's refusal to approve the
ticket immediately did not prevent the publication of a campaign pamphlet entitled *Address of the Cameron And Lincoln Club of the City of Chicago, Ill., To The People Of The
North West.* This final appeal in the pamphlet gives emphasis to Lincoln's anticipated contribution as a member of the
team: "The nomination of Mr. Lincoln will secure us the votes
of Illinois and Indiana, and we hope to carry Oregon and
California also. We *may* succeed with other candidates; with
Cameron and Lincoln, we *will.*"
Lincoln, when en route to New York for his speech at Cooper
Union, while passing through Philadelphia, was handed the
cards of Simon Cameron and David Wilmot but was unable to
contact them before leaving the city. Four months had passed
since they first solicited Lincoln's partnership on the ticket,
but apparently they feared he would make some agreement
about the Vice-Presidency with Seward, while in New York. It
is evident that a Seward-Lincoln ticket had already been pro-
posed.
It seems probable that the Young Men's Republican Union
may have had some specific reason for offering Lincoln 200
dollars to speak in New York, and very likely it had political
relevancy. His appearance was a rousing success and his
introduction to leading celebrities of the East opened up new
political horizons.
En route to New Hampshire to visit his son Robert, attending Exeter Academy, he was joined on the train by Frederick
Smyth who was to introduce him at Manchester. Lincoln had
been reading an address Seward had delivered before the United States Senate, and laying the paper down he said to
Smyth, "That speech will make Mr. Seward the next President of the United States." However, when Smyth came to the
conclusion of his introductory remarks, in presenting Lincoln he said: "The next President of the United States!"
An interesting phase of his New England trip was his pur-
posely passing through Massachusetts without making a
single speech. The state had already announced its support of
Seward, and apparently Lincoln did not wish to exhibit any
display of rivalry. Upon his return to New York, however, the
situation there seems to have changed. One of the young men
advised him: "When he came, they thought he might make a
good running mate for Seward, but after hearing him, they are
for him for President, regardless of what happens to Seward."
Succeeding the New York visit, Lincoln was the most
coveted Vice-Presidential candidate in the nation. These possible pairings were published in the press: Cameron and Lincoln, Seward and Lincoln, Chase and Lincoln, also Horace
Greeley's choice, Dayton and Lincoln, possibly others. In 1860
the Vice-Presidency beckoned Lincoln in preference to all
others. Lincoln had numerous advantages as a Vice-Presidential nominee (and, as it turned out, as a Presidential nominee). Unlike Salmon Chase and Simon Cameron, who had
bitter factional enemies in their home states, Lincoln's support in Illinois was secure and united, and the Republicans
needed Illinois. Unlike Cameron and Edward Bates, he was
sound on the slavery issue because he had steadily opposed
slavery as a moral evil. He had an instinct, too, for avoiding
controversial stands on unessential issues. Personally tem-
perate, Lincoln had avoided the prohibition agitation, especially when it became a hot issue in Illinois after 1853.
Despising the principles of the Know-Nothing agitation,
Lincoln avoided public condemnations of that party's
adherents. He also avoided the side issue of disobedience to
the Fugitive Slave Law.
Abraham's auspicious speaking itinerary in the East gave
a new impetus to his political aspirations considering the
forthcoming convention. David Davis appears to have assum-
ed the leadership of the voluntary group of Lincoln's supporters, combining their strength with the Chicago consti-
tuency. When the convention opened, it appeared like a one-
man show with Seward apparently so far ahead it forecast a

orrespondent put it this way: "Sena-
shoulders above all competitors, in
ıship, in authority, in influence, in
it a man for the Presidency." Horace
the balloting began, advised his *New*
that Seward would be victorious. It is
opposed to Seward.

making the ballots ready, causing
ɔting to the following day, was great-
uring the night considerable opposi-
generated. There were four, and pos-
ıich caused the dissatisfaction: 1. He
pport of important Pennsylvania. 2.
'ork Tribune were against him. 3.
ılature of New York while he was
rial manner of his delegates at the

ıad been the Vice-Presidential choice
nts gave him a great advantage over
. The first ballot gave Seward, 193,
ːward, 184, Lincoln, 181; third, Lin-
/2. No other candidate polled more

cing exhibits to support the supposi-
ːerted effort to procure the Vice-Presi-
incoln is a poster of his profile, now
ı National Life Foundation. On the
one-half by eleven inch lithograph is
ːorge William Curtis, a Seward dele-
ːhese prints were showered through
y after Mr. Lincoln's nomination."
rmation on the broadside to reveal
ıl candidate seeks, no name of the
, nor even the commercial printer.
s were not distributed until after Mr.
ıated for the Presidency, eliminates
ː were prepared as flyers to assist in
hief Executive office in the Nation.

ɔutors of the handbills were the
ıncoln committees. The fact that Cur-
comment in his inscribed note about
mplies that the Seward group had no
and no desire to boost Lincoln. The
e the Cameron-Lincoln loyalists, the
ı of Lincoln for the Vice-Presidency.
ere in Chicago where the "tousled
ade and used in producing the litho-
ıppearance would win votes in the
would have any value in garnering

ncoln convention group had nothing
ıe "tousled hair" flyer. The failure to
ː balloting for the Presidency almost
ɔf the lithograph with Lincoln's win-

ıe prints, however, does present a
ıcoln was a recognized contender for
ıe Wigwam Convention. The conclu-
ı, that inasmuch as Lincoln was the
ıe minor office of at least four of the
· is quite natural that if their first
ːes would swing to their junior part-
ıext choice, to salvage at least a part
here seems to have been little atten-
strength of these original supporters
Vice-President.

ı the Vice-Presidency did not cease
to the higher office. Quite naturally,
ɔle interest in the selection of his run-
e observed with more than common
ɔting for the nomination of the runner-
ıinee was none other than Cassius
been active in securing Lincoln's
lency and made a speech from which
ed: "It makes a great deal of differ-

ence to you whom you nominate . . . and it makes a much more
vital difference to us [Kentuckians]. . . . We call upon you to
nominate Abraham Lincoln, who knows us and understands
our aspirations."

Even before Lincoln had an opportunity to meet the Vice-
Presidential nominee, Hannibal Hamlin of Hamden, Maine,
there were certain press releases that made Lincoln anxious to
confer with his partner for the subsequent campaign. No
sooner had the names of the two successful candidates reached the East than some newspapers announced surprise and
dissatisfaction with the selections. One of the first reactions
was the arrangement of the names of the victorious contest-
ants. Many regarded Hamlin, an Eastern man, to be superior
to his Western associate and referred to the combination as
"The Upside-down Ticket."

While the new Presidential nominee may not have been as
well known as Hamlin, the name Lincoln was a household
word with the Hamlins. When Hannibal was but nine years
old, a lawyer from Worcester, Massachusetts, whose name
was Enoch Lincoln, came to live in the Hamlin home. Within
the next five years, Enoch was elected to Congress and next
became Governor of the State of Maine. He was Hannibal's
hero and eventually young Hamlin went to Congress and also
became Governor of Maine. Enoch Lincoln was a brother of
Levi Lincoln, the host of Abraham Lincoln at Worcester in
1848.

Inasmuch as this commentary has relied on current public
sentiment for a congenial atmosphere in which to develop this
argument, it would seem agreeable to bring it to a conclusion
in a similar fashion. The first person who put in writing a
declaration with reference to Abraham Lincoln's eventually
becoming President of the United States, was not a contemporary politician, but a "woman," Mary Todd of Lexington,
Kentucky. While she was living with her sister, Mrs. Ninian
Edwards at Springfield, Illinois, she became engaged to, and
later married, Abraham Lincoln, a member of the Illinois
Legislature. She wrote to one of her girl·friends, Margaret
Wickliffe, a daughter of the Governor of Kentucky, and after a
playful, but not a very flattering, description of the man of her
choice, she continued: "But I mean to make him to be President of the United States all the same. You will see that, as I
always told you, I will yet be the President's wife." Governor
Wickliffe, years later, after Lincoln had become President,
came across the letter and wrote on it this endorsement, "the
most remarkable letter ever written by one girl."

Researchers observing the intellectual training this young
lady acquired at Lexington, "The Athens of the West," are
agreed that her advanced formal education was superior to
that of any other First Lady who occupied the Executive Man-
sion up to the time of Mrs. Lincoln's tenure. The cultural
atmosphere which she created and nourished in her home,
barely mentioned by most of her biographers, contributed
greatly to the mental capacity of her husband.

We have observed that Lincoln was first a prospect for
national recognition by becoming the runner-up in the contest for the nomination of Vice-President in the first National
Republican Convention at Philadelphia in 1856. This nod, for
one of the two Chief Executive offices, may have contributed
more to his political advancement than we have recognized.

The multiple nods made to Lincoln as a Vice-Presidential
nominee in the campaign of 1860 are almost inconceivable. It
is doubtful if, ever before or since, one political aspirant has
been the first choice as a running mate by so many different
candidates for the Presidential nomination. Would it be pre-
sumtuous to assume that these unusual political alliances
may have been largely responsible in elevating him to the
office which his superiors coveted? As the dwindling hopes for
the first place on the ticket faded out, in order to salvage a part
of the preferred combination, would they not swing to their
junior partner rather than to one of their competitors?

The National Republican Convention, convening at the
Chicago Wigwam in 1860, had the unique distinction of
making a beckoning jesture to a Vice-Presidential hopeful
and announced that Abraham Lincoln of Illinois was the duly
elected Presidential nominee.

CONCERNING CLAY'S ATTITUDES TOWARD SELF DEFENSE:

"As soon as I stepped down frm the tabl on wh I stood, (to spk) Cyrus Tur... gave me the lie, and struck me. So knowing, as in Brown's case, wh this meant, I at one dw my knife. My arms we... seized, and my knife wrested from me—. Seeing I was to be m... I seized my Bowie-knife; and, catching it by the blade cut... two of my fngs to the ben I held it firmly for use. The blood my gushed violently from my side; and I felt the utts indignation. The way was opd... and I a... upon (Turner) and thrust the knife into his abdo-men, wh... meant death." (p. 18...)

IN DEFENSE OF "CASH," HENRY CLAY'S FINAL APPEAL TO THE JURY AFTER THE CLAY-BROWN FIGHT AT RUSSELL CAVE:

"Standing, as he did, with ... aiders or ab... and without popular sy... wh the fatal pistol of cop... ; n... pointed at his heart, would you hav... had him to do just what he did do—there stand in defense, or the fall? Or would you hav... had him meanly and cowardly fly? And, if he had not, he would not hav... been WORTHY OF THE NAME WHICH HE BEARS!"

Dedicated to the Revival of Interest

in the

LION OF WHITE HALL,

CASSIUS MARCELLUS CLAY,

One of Kentucky's Most Fascinating

Historical Figures

The Life Memoirs, Writings and Speeches, of

CASSIUS M. CLAY

OSCAR RUCKER, JR. OFFERS
The First Reprint Of The Original 1886 Edition
(Newly Indexed)

A rare autobiography by a Kentuckian wh was a friend and political contemporary of Ab... Lincoln and wh in his ni... years found time to be... on... of the most ardent abolitionists, much respected Bowie knife fighter, General in the Mexican War, orator, newspaper publisher, co-founder of Berea College, diplomat to the Czar of Russia, defender of the nation's capitol, author, and wh was also an indomitable romantic able to cause ladies hearts to flutter frm Me... City to St. Petersburg, as a prisoner of war as an Ambassador or as a landed Kentucky gentleman.

NOTE: If you plan to order, it is important that you do so immediately as this edition is to be limited to 2,000 copies, many of which have already been reserved. Although mailing will not begin until approximately November all checks or money orders of the prepublication subscribers that are made out to OSCAR RUCKER, JR.—SPECIAL ACCOUNT, will be held in escrow at the Berea National Bank, Berea, Kentucky, until shipment of the book is made.

Please send .... copy/copies of Cassius M. Clay's THE LIFE MEMOIRS, WRITINGS, AND SPEECHES OF CASSIUS M. CLAY which is illustrated with seven steel engravings and contains 600 pages plus the new index

to:

Name ....

Street .... City .... State .... Zip ....

Pre-publication subscription of $15.75 per copy includes 5% Ky. sales tax. After publication the cost per copy, including sales tax will be $21.00. (Original editions now cost $75.00 to $125.00 each.)

SEND ALL ORDERS TO: OSCAR RUCKER, JR., C.P.O. 1520, BEREA, KY. 40403

CONCERNING EDUCATION

"The vast ... of the ... ... (1885) is more ... subject at ... and at ... impotent.'" p. 54

CONCERNING A GIFT OF LAND AND MONEY TO FOUND BEREA COLLEGE:

"In ... Berea ... Rev. ... G. Fee, wh... the law—to me ... ... to be released." p. 148-149)

CONCERNING CLAY'S INTEREST DURING THE ...

... Zambonin ... of Henry's movements. ...

CONCERNING CLAY'S INTEREST IN A BIG SENORITA:

"I ... to ... the ... Lolu's ... lattice porch. She was ... ... stove, an... and kissed—me? Not at all. ..." (p. 160

CONCERNING HIS FATHER:

"He ... a ... life ... but ... Having ... Some of ... ... he buck." p. 45

CONCERNING THE SURPRISE OF A SLAVE:

"In ... of an iron ... Yet in ... in ... in my ... see ... hands ... a Texas ... My ... Devil ... Was I ... so politically guilty? ... chickens. ... to a ... deadly ... Cause'." (p. 28)

CONCERNING RELIGION AND ABOLITION:

"There was a ... (at ...) ... in New Haven Sound. ... just as I ... ... of ... G. Fee, ... no ... Institution," and I ... Devil ... SILENT, at ... So, if I ... ... with slavery." (p. 57)

During his ... 810 to 183, ... met ... by ... of ... 1800's. Among ... "Lion" as he ... Van Buren, ... Robert ... M. H. Seward, J ... Prince ... G. Z. ..., ... Ulysses S. ... Fee, ... are ... Legend ... by "Cash's" ... ... wife ... "Memoirs," ... M. Clay's ... Kentucky ...

FROM THE PREFACE

"The ... of ... of Henry ... ... hatreds." ... of ... ... of Slavery in ... ... thaw of ... ... But ... or Empire— is ... forever. ... Can ...

CONCERNING HIS HOME—WHITE HALL:

"I ... in ... with I was ... It is ... with heavy ... ... to ... 1861; ... the ... after ..." (p. 19)

CONCERNING EDUCATION

"The ... of ... intellect than no ... at all, in the greatest ... ... The ... ... failure to grasp the subject at ..., ... and at ... impotent!" (p. 54)

CONCERNING A GIFT OF LAND AND MONE... TO FOUND BEREA COLLEGE:

"In the ... seeing that the ... ... were ... and the ... ... into the ... ... their benefit. I had ... ... of a ... ... to the) Berea College. So I wrote to my ... friend, the Rev. John G. Fee, ... regarded all men as brothers and ... God and the law—to ... ... by his efforts, now growing into a great and ... college, where white and ... ..., men, are ... ... terms." (p. 212)

CONCERNING CLAY'S CAPTURE DURING THE MEXICAN WAR:

"Henry got a fair start before the ... ... draw their carbines and fire. Col. Zambonin ... ordered them ... to be ... and. But ordered the ... ... to lie ... they prompt... and I ... had that the men were ... and fled, seeing all safe from danger, ordered m... at ... to be released." (pp. ...)

CONCERNING CLAY'S INTEREST IN A YOUNG SENORITA:

"I tried to get the ... to ... join me in sortie; but they all ... But all things are ... ... a man is in the ... So, pro... curing a sombrero and serape I was ready for ..., having no ... gun but a ... The guard, of course, as we were on parole, had order to pass ... ... or on ... out. Lolu's cottage was ... ... by tropical ... ... I saw warning. She was sitting ... in her ... ... porch, and ... caressing her pet ... ... This girl was about eighteen ... of mor... stature above the ... Indian ... ... ull in person. As I ... in her arose in ... na, but ... can be recognized me, the ... an as the ... through a ... ... dropping her ..., ... me, with ... arms and kissed—me? Not at all. The parrot." (p. 160)

CONCERNING HIS FATHER:

"He ... struck me a blow for ... ... imported a fine merino buck, he had him tied to a tree; ..., whilst he was at ..., int..., seeing the ... a title ... But my ... ... in the act of inviting a trial of ... of ... with the ... ... But my ... ... returning, and seeing my danger, ... the flat of his ... ... did me ... farther than the ... ... of my ... ... will ... me Some of the ... of my ... ... after ... ... on ... this in after-life, that my father ... ..., for my ... had ... so hard for the buck." (p. 45)

CONCERNING THE SURPRISE OF A SLAVE:

"In the early ..., the ... of an iron collar was used to prevent the ... from running ... Nothing ... the degradation of the ... ... more than his ..., with ... was generally ... before my ..., Yet in Lexington, in 1845, whilst I edited ... HERE, ..., the ... I ... my ... and ... out to see the ... ult of ... of ... in my ... ... To my surprise, a Negro man had both ... of The ... ... He belonged to a ... ... man ... who ran a ... ... was poorly fed and that he ought to ... ... but to her face. I told ... with ... indignation, that he ought ... to ... to me, his own ... friend of his ..., to ... To ... ... him he replied, 'Mars' ..., I did not ... it ... you had hurt me.' This reasoning was not at all ... ... but the low ... ... at a few rays through the ..., the ..., and I saw the bright prongs of a ... collar as long, on ... side of his ..., as the ... of a ... ... in my rage, ... at first ... ... —standing ... ... I ... ... into ... ... and I let the ... fellow go with all the ... Was I not ... ... guilty? ... ... nerved me to a ... ... warfare against the 'Lost Cause'." (p. 28)

FROM THE PREFACE

"The misfortune of the ... Henry ... and ..., including ..., is that the ... of great parties for immortal hatreds."

"Every man ... ... be ... ... by his gr... all ... — but by the ... and honors of office ... ... to the triumph of the ... which ... add to ... ... his. In the history gratitude. ... the ... law of Slavery in his ... ... in the judgement of my, ... a ... ... out from monarchy by great ... ... and ..., at, in the course of ... ... we may ... return to it again. But ..., ... Republic or Empire — is gone forever. ... ... the ... of ... ... secured to the ... ... by ...." (p. 28)

CONCERNING HIS HOME—WHITE HALL:

"I ... ... in the ... in ... I was born. It is a ... ... with ... by range work of Kentucky marble and grey ... ... of imperfect Corinthian and Doric ... It was ... to after 1861; but the old building, after the ... ... was preserved ... ..., ... at that day, though the ... were ... my ... to the ... ... were ... unbroken by the ..., The ..., and ... ah, Kentucky coffee ..., the ..., it was ... ... rose at ..., ... to ... ... a limb." (p. 19)

CONCERNING RELIGION AND ABOLITION:

"There was a ... revival in ... ... year (at ...). I was ... by the ... ... a ... of course, ... as I did ... on trust; but ... I began to read the ... ... they all around me ... We clergy, with the ? ... of Fee, ... standing for slavery as a ... ... I had no ... ... with men with ... a creed; and I preferred, if God was on the ... ..., to ... with the Devil ..., for he was ... ... in person. As I ... it ... and ... rote hard things against the ..., it was ... ... were the false prophets, ... it was ... ... to destroy with slavery?" (p. 57)

"I was born in Madison County, Kentucky, United States of America, October 19, 1810, on the uplands of Tate's and Jack's Creeks, near the Kentucky River."

"… my first duty in Russia was to keep the Czar, if possible, on the Union side; and therefore, my business was to please. I was introduced to the Princess; and she invited me to call and see her …"

He was romantic, mysterious, volatile and violent. The son of Kentucky's largest slave owner, Cassius Marcellus Clay would have seemed an unlikely candidate for leadership in the struggle for emancipation. Yet his conscience, courage and uncompromising ideals would allow him no other path, no matter what the cost.

In this one-hour dramatic presentation adapted from Clay's *Memoirs*, Steve Wise is The Lion of White Hall, using Clay's own haunting, poetic words to relive his youth, his promising political career, and his dangerous antislavery campaign. From publisher of the abolitionist newspaper, *The True American*, to prisoner in a Mexican jail, Cassius Marcellus Clay was a complex, controversial figure, and Steve Wise offers a rare, insightful portrayal of the man at the center of the storm.

Though he walked with kings as a friend to Lincoln and Ambassador to Russia, Clay spent his later years alone with his memories – pacing the chambers and corridors of White Hall like a caged lion – deserted by his friends and divorced by his wife of 45 years.

In *The Lion of White Hall*, Steve Wise has created a powerful, personal portrayal that goes beyond the historical documents, behind the factual accounts, and unearths the heart and soul of one of the most fascinating men in Kentucky history. Make your reservations now, for a theatrical experience you'll never forget!

Following each performance, Mr. Wise invites the audience to join him in a discussion which brings the colorful and memorable life of Cassius Marcellus Clay into vivid historical perspective. Entitled The Legendary Lion of White Hall, *the presentation features more than a hundred slides – many from private collections never before seen by the general public. Sometimes fantastic, frequently humorous, always intriguing and provocative, it is easily the most comprehensive visual study ever assembled of Clay and his times.*

THE TRUE AMERICAN.

"I was born in Madison County, Kentucky, United States of America, October 19, 1810, on the uplands of Tate's and Jack's Creeks, near the Kentucky River."

"...my first duty in Russia was to keep the Czar, if possible, on the Union side; and therefore, my business was to please. I was introduced to the Princess; and she invited me to call and see her..."

He was romantic, mysterious, volatile and violent. The son of Kentucky's largest slave owner, Cassius Marcellus Clay would have seemed an unlikely candidate for leadership in the struggle for emancipation. Yet his conscience, courage and uncompromising ideals would allow him no other path, no matter what the cost.

In this one-hour dramatic presentation adapted from Clay's *Memoirs*, Steve Wise is The Lion of White Hall using Clay's own haunting, poetic words to relive his youth, his promising political career, and his dangerous anti-slavery campaign. From publisher of the abolitionist newspaper, *The True American*, to prisoner in a Mexican jail, Cassius Marcellus Clay was a complex, controversial figure, and Steve Wise offers a rare, insightful portrayal of the man at the center of the storm.

Though he walked with kings as a friend to Lincoln and Ambassador to Russia, Clay spent his later years alone with his memories – pacing the chambers and corridors of White Hall like a caged lion – deserted by his friends and divorced by his wife of 45 years.

In *The Lion of White Hall*, Steve Wise has created a powerful, personal portrayal that goes beyond the historical documents, behind the factual accounts, and unearths the heart and soul of one of the most fascinating men in Kentucky history. Make your reservations now, for a theatrical experience you'll never forget!

Following each performance, Mr. Wise invites the audience to join him in a discussion which brings the colorful and memorable life of Cassius Marcellus Clay into vivid historical perspective. Entitled The Legendary Lion of White Hall, the presentation features more than a hundred slides – many from private collections never before seen by the general public. Sometimes fantastic, frequently humorous, always intriguing and provocative, it is easily the most comprehensive visual study ever assembled of Clay and his times.

Steve Wise as

**The Lion of White Hall:
Cassius Marcellus Clay**

**White Hall State
Historic Site
Richmond, Kentucky**

**Thursdays, Fridays
& Saturdays
at 8:15 p.m.
July 6-August 12**

Tickets: $5.00

For Reservations, call:
Richmond Tourism
606-623-0759

This program has been produced through the generous
assistance of:

**The Kentucky State Parks
The Kentucky Center for the Arts
Richmond Tourism Commission**

"...yesterday ... I was denounced as a disturber of the peace – yesterday we were threatened with the halter – today we speak in the capital of the State, and we may speak and be heard in every part of the State. The tongue is again free to speak the language of the heart."

"The two great nations, as Napoleon seemed to foresee, will eventually be, in the world's history, Russia and the United States ...."

"Lincoln gave me a most patient hearing ... I flattered myself, when Lincoln listened to my animated appeal for universal liberty for more than two hours, that I sowed there seed which in due time bore fruit."

You won't want to miss *The Lion of White Hall*, as Cassius Marcellus Clay lives again in a dramatic, one-man portrayal by noted actor/playwright *Steve Wise*. This riveting performance will take you to the most turbulent time in Kentucky history and introduce you to the fiery, controversial man whose tempestuous life and exploits in the battle for emancipation shook the state and the nation – and led him to bitter personal tragedy.

Act now, while seats are still available!

.

CPSIA information can be obtained
at www.ICGtesting.com
Printed in the USA
BVHW04*1221080818
523683BV00043B/223/P

9 780484 612128